AI
FOR
BEGINNERS

Skeptics Guide

Automate tasks, streamline your life, expand your earnings,

Fun, easy exercises for anyone,

NO TECH SKILLS needed!

Contents

Thank you!

My wife, who tolerates me.

The Early Reading team, thank you for your feedback and early input.

Brian, Cathy, and Janice thank you for reviewing line by line.

My mom for many reasons beyond not killing me while torturing her throughout my teen years.

Introduction

My AI story & Journey: how I was introduced to AI on the Canary Islands.

There were 7 of us on a 9-day sailing cruise beginning in Malaga, Spain, ending in the Canary Islands. It was my friend Camille's 60th birthday celebration. Camille spoke to me about the trip long before, mentioning how it is different traveling with a group of people versus alone, as I usually do, and not worrying if I didn't want to do the same excursions as the group. Given it was her memorable trip, I told her she would hear two things come out of my mouth the entire trip, "*That sounds great.*" or, "*I think I'll stay on board.*" I planned to stay after they left Madrid to see Guernica, a painting by Picasso, some of Salvador Dali's work, and eat.

On the morning of the ninth day in the Canary Islands, we debarked the ship, found a place to store our bags, and began our sightseeing journey. Camille pulled out a piece of paper with a list of things to do. I have traveled with Camille many times. I plan, and she has someone else plan. I asked where the suggestions came from. "I typed what to do in the Canary Islands if you have 8 hours into ChatGPT, and this is what it gave me."

I was floored. In an instant, all the hours, days, weeks, and months of planning every trip I have ever taken - 18 days in Hawaii for our honeymoon, every road trip, our trip to Italy for two weeks, a 27-day RV trip across the United States and back during COVID, London, Amsterdam, several trips to Canada, an Alaskan cruise, cruise to Cuba, Portland every other year since my son was born I planned out our activities. That planning resulted in finding OMSI (Oregon Museum of Science and Industry) with their children's interactive section, where he spent hours with a massive smile on his face for possibly 12 years. Including the Churchill Underground in London, the WWII Museum in New Orleans, and other great experiences for our son and us as he was growing up. I do not regret finding those events and places, and I have spent possibly more hours researching to find the perfect things to do than even I can imagine - all wasted time. I am being a bit dramatic for effect.

It was a great day packed with beautiful sights and experiences. The suggestions from ChapGPT blew me away because I was an AI skeptic, and it would ruin life as we know it. The next day at breakfast, most, if not all, had cured Jamone sandwiches and superb coffee. I asked Camille what was on the agenda for the day. You already know what happened. The list of AI "things to do if you have a free day in Madrid" appeared. It was one of the most extraordinary days with my best friends and their spouses I have ever had. Museums, sights of interest, suggested places to eat. I didn't read the list, so I do not know if it said reservations are recommended at one of the oldest restaurants. We would have had reservations if I had been doing the research, but I digressed. That restaurant wasn't the vibe of the day either; it was cool to look at as a sight but not for a casual lunch, so AI got that right, too. I would have canceled our reservations or killed the day's vibe with the must-do item I researched.

As soon as I got home, I started looking at AI. ChatGPT was my first paid service, and I got my money's worth. I began playing with email content suggestions, such as the emails you do not want to write. It increased my productivity that day. I would type something like "edit this email to x, y, or z" or "edit to be professional & concise, and engaging." I can be long-winded when there is no call for it. I would type that before my draft, and a great-sounding email would present itself in seconds. I would always have to edit and tweak, and I had the draft of a professional email right there versus spending hours or days lamenting before starting to write. Previously, after drafting a critical email, I would ask someone for their thoughts, especially if the stakes were high when I felt immense pressure to perform on a level needed to produce the intended outcome (a sale) or if I was just stuck. ChatGPT was a game-changer for me.

I then pointed ChatGPT at marketing for the high school marching band. We raised over $20,000.00 that school year! I created email campaigns and social media announcement campaigns to market our first two car washes (One carwash raised just over $2k, the other just under $2k). There were a ton of parents and student volunteers that made executing possible. Besides the band parents giving time and money, the marketing took us outside our school bubble into the community. Without community engagement, we would have raised much less. All fundraising activities I marketed with ChatGPT were very successful.

The band has a brand new sponsor program, a resurfaced billboard, new sponsor signs on that billboard, and a positive cash flow in the first year. The billboard project was completed in a month with the help of AI. It's an easy sell if you reach outside the parents of band students. AI suggested a three-year discount for sponsors, so the first year has already generated future revenue for the next two school years! All that was invented with the assistance of AI.

Law enforcement officials told me that present-day criminals ignore old-school alarm systems. You know, the ones you set off and then get a call and ask for your secret word. I never remember that word, either. They tell me cameras are one of the best things for catching criminals. Possibly not for the reasons you are thinking. Getting footage of criminals in the act, maybe a piece of a license plate, if they rob more than one place in an evening, all that footage will help in apprehending the criminals. I have cameras all over the outside and inside of my home. I am about to install a smoke/CO_2 detector in my house and attempt to have it dial the authorities when smoke is detected, with AI replacing my $35-a-month alarm monitoring company, which I keep for fire-only.

At home, we have smart thermostats that are adaptable to save us energy. I have not ventured down that self-adapting path yet. Getting them programmed was almost out of my scope. It was all user error—me and my mistakes in not following instructions. You know the drill: guy knowledge is better than any instruction manual except when it's not. I was making it more complicated than it was. This is true with everything AI I have come into contact with. I make it more difficult.

There are a ton of books out there that go much deeper into AI than this book. All you have to do is search those words, and you'll get many results. When I slow it down and digest it one thing at a time, it has become my best employee ever, said jokingly, but it doesn't get mad at me if I ask it something after hours.

I wrote this book in bite-sized chunks with a guide and exercises to do at your own pace and comfort level, with you, the novice, beginner, and skeptic, in mind. If you are curious about AI, this book is meant for beginners. If you are an expert, at the very least, my stories can entertain you and give you a good laugh.

Chapter One

Understanding AI Basics

What is AI? – Unraveling the Basics

So, what exactly is AI? In the simplest terms, Artificial Intelligence is a branch of computer science that aims to create machines capable of mimicking human intelligence. Think of it as teaching computers how to learn, reason, perceive, infer, communicate, and make decisions to solve problems, much like humans do. AI is not just about robots; it's about integrating software with the ability to think intelligently. The scope of AI is vast—it stretches from the apps that recommend what to stream next to more complex systems like autonomous vehicles navigating traffic.

Brief History

The concept of AI isn't new. It dates back to the mid-20th century when the brilliant mathematician Alan Turing posed a provocative question: "Can machines think?" This question sparked a flurry of scientific activity. In 1950, Turing devised the Turing Test to determine whether a machine is intelligent. Can a machine engage in a conversation without the human realizing it is a machine? If yes, the machine passed the test. In the 21st century, AI has evolved from a theory into an integral part of our lives—all thanks to advances in computing power and data storage availability.

Types of AI: Let's break down AI into some small chunks.

Artificial Intelligence (AI) encompasses a variety of types and applications, each designed to perform specific tasks or solve particular problems. Here are the main types of AI:

1. Reactive Machines: Definition: A basic form of AI that reacts to current inputs but does not store memories or past experiences to influence future decisions.

Examples: IBM's Deep Blue chess computer, which can identify pieces on the chessboard and make predictions but does not learn from past games.

2. Limited Memory: Definition: AI systems that can store past experiences and use them to make better decisions in the future. They have a limited memory and can recall information for a short period.

Examples: Self-driving cars that observe the speed and direction of other vehicles over time to make better driving decisions.

3. Theory of Mind Definition: An advanced form of AI that understands humans' emotions, beliefs, and thoughts, allowing AI to interact socially.

Examples: AI research is ongoing in this area, aiming to create robots that can understand and predict human behavior.

4. Self-Aware AI Definition: The most advanced form of AI, which has its own consciousness and self-awareness. It can understand its own state and form its own ideas.

Examples: This type of AI currently exists only in theory and science fiction.

5. Artificial Narrow Intelligence (ANI): Definition: AI designed and trained to perform a specific task. It operates within a limited context and is also known as weak AI.

Examples: Voice assistants like Siri and Alexa and recommendation systems on Netflix and Amazon.

6. Artificial General Intelligence (AGI): Definition: AI with the ability to understand, learn, and apply knowledge across a wide range of tasks, similar to human intelligence. It is also known as strong AI.

Examples: AGI does not yet exist, but it is a goal for AI researchers.

7. Artificial Superintelligence (ASI): Definition: AI that surpasses human intelligence in all aspects, including creativity, problem-solving, and social intelligence.

Examples: ASI remains a hypothetical concept and is a topic of debate among researchers and ethicists.

8. Machine Learning (ML): Definition: A subset of AI that involves training algorithms to make predictions or decisions based on data. ML models improve over time with more data

    Examples: Spam email filtering, fraud detection, and recommendation engines.

9. Deep Learning (DL): Definition: A subset of ML that uses neural networks with many layers (deep networks) to analyze various factors of data (another way of referring to categorical variables). DL is particularly good at recognizing patterns such as image and speech recognition and natural language processing.

10. Natural Language Processing (NLP): Definition: AI that enables computers to understand, interpret, and naturally respond to human language.

    Examples: Chatbots, language translation services, sentiment analysis.

11. Expert Systems: Definition: AI is designed to solve complex problems by reasoning through bodies of knowledge, represented mainly as if-then rules rather than statistical models.

    Examples are medical diagnosis systems and technical support systems.

Each type of AI has unique capabilities and applications, making AI a versatile tool for solving problems across different industries.

Real-world Examples: To see AI in action, you don't need to go anywhere, look around your house, or in your pocket. Your email's spam filter? That's AI at work, sorting out junk mail or your smartphone's personal assistant - be it Siri, Alexa, or Google Assistant - answering questions and following commands, all powered by AI. These tools learn from the data we feed them (like voice commands or written texts) to better predict and react to our requests. Do you have a device on your kitchen counter, bedroom, playroom, or children's room that talks to you?

Interactive Element: Quiz

Let's have some fun and see how well you can spot AI in your day! Here's a quick quiz:

- Does your phone auto-correct your spelling mistakes?

- Do you play a video game, and the characters seem to predict your moves?

- Does your online shopping platform recommend products?

- Can your car park itself?

If you answered yes to any of these, congratulations, you're already interacting with AI!

By breaking AI down into these bite-sized pieces, the hope is to educate you on the tech and show its practical, everyday benefits. As we progress, keep in mind that AI, at its core, is here to make our lives *easier and more efficient.*

Differentiating AI, Machine Learning, and Deep Learning: Imagine you're learning to cook. At first, you follow recipes. Then, you start tweaking them based on past cooking experiences. Finally, you're whipping up dishes based on subtle flavors and textures you've come to understand. These stages show how you evolve from strictly following instructions to making nuanced decisions based on a deep understanding of cooking. Similarly, AI, machine learning, and deep learning represent different depths of data comprehension and decision-making capabilities in technology.

Clarify the Differences:

AI is the umbrella term for machines designed to mimic human intelligence. It's like the entire cookbook on how to cook. Under this vast umbrella, computers learn from data to improve their tasks without being explicitly programmed for every step. It's like using your cooking experiences to tweak recipes or even create new ones.

A subset of machine learning goes even deeper. It uses complex algorithms to analyze data, recognize patterns, and make decisions. Think of it as understanding not just the recipe but each ingredient's flavor profile and how they combine in various culinary conditions.

Dive deeper into machine learning, and you'll see it's all about algorithms and step-by-step computational procedures. These algorithms use historical data as input to predict new output values. Think of spam filters in your email. They learn from various signals, like which emails you open and which you quickly trash. Over time, the system learns enough to predict which incoming emails are spam. It's a continuous cycle of feedback and improvement.

Deep learning is like having a master chef's intuition. It involves neural networks—a series of algorithms modeled loosely after the human brain—that learn from large amounts of data. These networks recognize patterns and features in layers. The first layer might only see individual pixels of an image, but deeper layers recognize edges, shapes, and ultimately complex objects like faces or even emotions on those faces. It's about going beyond the obvious, delving into the subtleties of data that even skilled humans might miss.

By understanding the layers of complexity, you can begin to see how much goes into AI and how many conveniences it powers. From the personal assistant in your smartphone to recommendation engines suggesting your next favorite movie or product, AI is there, making things simpler and more personalized. As we peel back these layers, technology becomes less of an abstract concept and more of a tangible, understandable tool that is less about machines taking over the world and more about them enhancing our human experiences in ways we are just beginning to explore and understand.

How AI is Changing Our Daily Lives

If you wake up to the soft glow of your smart lamp gradually brightening, If you wake up early and your smartwatch asks if you want to skip your morning wake alarm—it's AI easing you into your day. This seamless integration of artificial intelligence into our everyday devices transforms our daily routines in ways we're just beginning to appreciate. Our smartphones are our loyal sidekicks, and we possibly spend more time with them than any one human. They are packed with AI-driven capabilities: voice-activated prompts and predictive text to finish sentences better than our best friends or spouses. Smart home assistants are ready to adjust thermostats, play music, and order groceries or fast food with a simple voice command. These devices learn from our routines and preferences, adapting to make life smoother, providing an opportunity to be less task-oriented and available to connect with and spend time on people, places, and things that require our full attention—hobbies, advancing at work, time to read or research. Automating our mundane tasks will free up time for the things that matter most to us.

AI's influence on consumer services can't be overstated. Have you ever wondered how Netflix seems to think it knows just the right series to suggest? Or how does Amazon magically line up all those 'you might also like' products? That's AI working behind the scenes. AI tailors personalized recommendations by analyzing your previous interactions, purchases, and browsing times. This isn't just convenient—it's setting new standards for customer service globally. Online shopping isn't just about buying anymore; it's about discovering products in a way that feels personal and human, even though algorithms power it.

AI's impact is profound and promises even greater advances. Tools like predictive diagnostics use AI to analyze medical data and predict health risks before they become evident. Imagine a routine doctor's visit where AI tools quickly analyze your vitals and genetic information, providing a personalized health report that flags any potential health issues months or even years before symptoms appear.

I wish AI were as effective in diagnosing lung cancer as it is with prostate and breast cancer. Imagine if my physical that revealed a suspicious spot in my left lung was found years earlier. I might not have gone through being treated for lung cancer with months of chemo, a lobectomy to remove my lower left lung, and a month of radiation. Imagine if it had been detected before and treated with a simple outpatient procedure. Or if Dna-tailored medication had been available before the spot was visible to the human eye. AI can pick up what the human eye can not and identify and diagnose cancer earlier. An early intervention gives people a better chance of survival. The numbers are improving, just not as fast a rate where AI cancer detection is fully implemented, such as P.A.I.G.E. prostate and breast cancer screening.

AI pushes boundaries in everything, from traffic management to self-driving cars. AI-driven logistics platforms optimize routes and loads in real time, saving millions in fuel costs and reducing carbon footprints. Self-driving cars are here, learning and adapting to real-world conditions, promising a future where traffic jams and driving accidents "could" become relics of the past. These cars use complex AI algorithms to navigate, make split-second decisions, and even learn from other vehicles around them, all while keeping safety at the forefront.

AI is present in our daily lives in countless ways, from when we wake up and go to bed to how we shop, travel, and manage our health. It is becoming an indispensable part of our lives, and we might not have even noticed it until it suddenly seemed everywhere.

AI Myths Debunked: What AI Is and Isn't

You're not alone if you've ever pictured AI as a sinister robot plotting world domination or a magical genie that can solve all of humanity's problems with a snap of its digital fingers. Hollywood and sensational headlines are known for stirring up undue fear and unrealistic expectations. It's time to set the record straight about what AI really is, what it can do, and where it's still learning the ropes.

AI is not about creating malevolent robots to take over the world. Yes, AI might beat the world champion at chess or suggest which new TV show might keep you glued to your couch. That AI could suddenly turn conscious and rogue is a thrilling plot for a movie, but it is far-reaching. AI operates within a very defined set of algorithms and data sets provided by human programmers. Why the mix-up? Often, what's dubbed AI is simply automation – machines programmed to perform repetitive tasks efficiently. Understanding this helps us understand the technology and reduces the fear factor dramatically.

So, what can AI do? Today's AI excels at processing information and identifying patterns at speeds beyond human capabilities. It powers recommendation engines, helps diagnose diseases by analyzing medical imaging, and improves home energy efficiency through smart thermostats. However, AI is not the end-all. Its capabilities are bounded by the data it's trained on and the tasks it's designed to perform. AI trained to detect fraud in financial transactions is clueless about diagnosing patients in a hospital.

As we integrate AI into our lives, ethical considerations concern everyone. How do we ensure AI is fair? What happens if it makes a mistake? Who is responsible? For example, if an AI hiring tool develops biases based on the data it's fed, it could unfairly reject job candidates. Addressing these issues involves careful design, continuous monitoring, and incorporating diverse data and perspectives to mitigate bias. It's a complex challenge requiring cooperation from every touch point, from developers, users, and regulators alike, setting the stage for how to guide AI development responsibly.

Fact vs. Fiction

- **Myth:** AI can learn and evolve on its own.

  - **Fact:** AI requires humans to set it up and provide it with the data.

AI's learning is not like human learning. It's more about adjusting to patterns it recognizes in data. If data changes or is biased, AI's outputs will be skewed.

Another popular **myth** is that AI can replace humans in all tasks. The truth is more nuanced. AI can replace humans in specific tasks, especially repetitive and data-intensive tasks. Jobs that require emotional intelligence, creativity, and complex decision-making _**are still better handled by humans.**_ Understanding these limitations helps us better integrate AI into society, ensuring it augments human capabilities rather than replaces them.

The Building Blocks of AI: Data, Algorithms, and Models

Imagine you're baking a cake—maybe a three-layer chocolate ganache with whipped cream frosting. Now, to whip up this masterpiece, you'll need:

#1: the right ingredients (the data),

#2: a good recipe (the algorithm),

#3: and the correct baking technique (the model),

This culinary trio operates similarly, crafting solutions rather than sweets.

The cornerstone of all AI systems is data. Like the cake, quality depends on the freshness of the eggs and the cream richness of your chocolate. The effectiveness of an AI system is all about what humans give it and the quality, quantity, and variety of its data. Quality data must be accurate, complete, and relevant; more data isn't always better. Quantity, or the amount of data, also plays a critical role—the more data an AI system has, the better it can learn and adapt. However, it's the variety that often makes a big difference. This involves collecting data from various sources—images, texts, clicks, etc.— to give the AI a well-rounded understanding of the task. For instance, training an AI system designed to recognize speech with voices that vary by accent, pitch, and tone is vital to ensure it performs well in real-world scenarios.

Algorithms—are the recipes for our AI system, guiding the process of turning our raw data (ingredients) into actions or decisions (our delicious cake). An algorithm is a set of rules or instructions for solving a problem or completing a task. In AI, algorithms make decisions and learn from data. They adjust their strategy based on feedback received to improve performance. A navigation app like Google Maps uses algorithms to analyze the speed of traffic flow. By continually learning from new data—like road closures or traffic speed—it refines its route recommendations to ensure you reach your destination quickly.

AI models are frameworks through which algorithms operate—they define how an algorithm processes data to make decisions. Think of them as the specific baking techniques in the kitchen analogy. The most common types of AI models are decision trees, support vector machines, and neural networks.

Decision trees are like flowcharts that lead to a decision based on a series of choices — akin to deciding whether to add more sugar based on whether your mix is sweet enough. Here is a simple diagram.

Is the person fit?

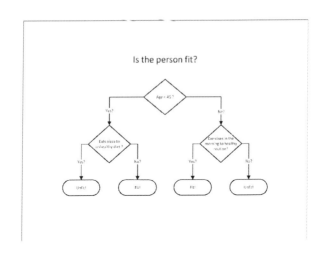

SVMs support vector machines that are used for classification tasks. Imagine trying to split your batter into layers perfectly; find the best 'line' (or hyperplane in higher dimensions) that divides the data into categories.

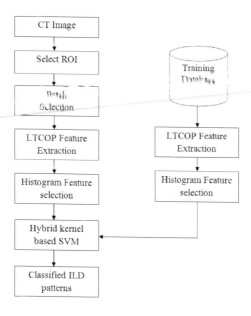

Neural networks, inspired by the human brain, are interconnected nodes (or neurons) that recognize patterns and make predictions based on large amounts of data.

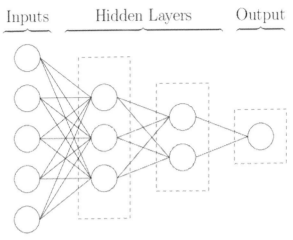

Seeing these models in action helps clarify their utility. Take the financial industry, for example, where AI models detect fraudulent transactions. Decision trees could determine whether a transaction is fraudulent based on transaction amount, location, and timing.

In healthcare, support vector machines classify cells in medical imaging as malignant or benign, which is crucial for early cancer detection. Meanwhile, neural networks play a significant role in customer service, powering chatbots that can understand and respond to customer queries by recognizing patterns in text data.

Enhancing user experience, streamlining operations, making critical decisions, and deploying models based on accurate data and algorithms will lead to advancements and innovations across all industries,

Understanding Neural Networks: A Non-Technical Approach

Think of your brain as a garden and your thoughts as flowers. If thoughts are flowers, then data points are the flowers of neural networks. Instead of paths, they use algorithms to guide their learning. It might seem an odd way to see if that simplifies the complexities of neural networks, the heart of AI, and its power.

Neural networks are directed by our understanding of the human brain's architecture. As our brain uses neurons interconnected by synapses to transmit and process information, neural networks use algorithms to handle this process. The primary goal? To recognize patterns and solve problems. But unlike our brains, neural networks are usually designed to address specific issues, such as translating languages, recognizing speech, or identifying objects in photos.

A neural network is structured in layers, each consisting of units called neurons. The hidden layers process this data through a complex web of computational neurons that adjust and learn over time. Finally, the output layer delivers the final decision or prediction, such as identifying the face in a photo or the words in a voice command.

Think of it as a multi-layered cake. The bottom layer (input) is your basic sponge — essential but unexciting. The hidden layers are where all the exciting stuff happens: cream, fruit, and flavorings that interact in complex ways to create something delicious. The top layer (output) is the icing and decoration — the part everyone sees and interacts with.

Chapter Two

AI in Everyday Life

Have you ever had that "Oh, so that's how it works!" moment when you finally figure out how to use a feature on your smartphone you've ignored for ages? Brace yourself for a few more of those as we dive into how AI is getting stuff done through our most loyal daily companion—the smartphone. It's like discovering a superhero has been living quietly in your pocket!

Smartphones and AI:

Your smartphone, that sleek little gadget that almost feels like an extension of your hand, is a powerhouse of AI-driven features. Let's start with predictive text. Have you noticed how your phone seems to know what you're about to type? That's AI in action. AI algorithms analyze your writing habits and vocabulary to predict what word you'll type next. It's like having a tiny mind-reader who helps speed up your texting. But it's not just about saving a few seconds; predictive text also reduces typos and can help improve your grammar.

Then there's facial recognition technology, which is common now. Your phone will unlock automatically when you look at it. AI analyzes the unique features of your face, creating a model that it uses to recognize you among thousands of people. It's not just convenient; it's also a step forward in personalized security.

Voice recognition like Siri, Google Assistant, and Bixby understand and execute your voice commands using AI to understand your speech patterns, learn your preferences, and even pick up on your unique accent, making interacting with your device more natural and intuitive.

One of the most practical applications of AI on your smartphone that you might not even be aware of is battery life management. AI optimizes how your phone uses its battery. It uses the data from your usage patterns—like when you typically charge your phone, which apps are used most, and at what times of day—AI adjusts your phone's energy consumption. This might mean closing background apps you're not using or reducing screen brightness when you typically don't use your phone. The result? Your phone stays alive longer.

Lastly, let's consider security enhancements—after all, your phone is packed with personal data, activity history, and much more. AI uses features like anomaly detection, which alerts you to unusual activity that could indicate a security breach, such as an attempt to access your phone from an unrecognized location.

Adaptive authentication: Your phone's security adapts based on the risk level of the action being taken. You might need a simple swipe to open your music app, but you will need a fingerprint or facial recognition to access banking apps. Some financial institutions' apps do not allow facial recognition or storing your password. Two-factor authentication and authenticator apps are prevalent in many applications today. These are all designed to prevent your apps from being hacked.

Your smartphone, equipped with AI, isn't just a device; it's a tool that adapts, learns, and anticipates your needs to make life easier. AI is there, enhancing every swipe, tap, and press. As we continue to explore AI's roles, remember this technology isn't just about the future; it's here now.

AI in Your Home:

The idea of a 'smart home' used to sound like something straight out of a futuristic movie. It's not the future anymore; it's what could be happening in your living room and kitchen right now. AI has sneakily made it into our homes, making them more intelligent and efficient. Take smart thermostats and lighting systems. These aren't just fancy gadgets. They can be tools that adjust your home environment for comfort and energy efficiency. Imagine a thermostat that learns your schedule and temperature preferences—knowing to crank up the heat before you get home. And those smart lights? They dim or brighten based on the time of day or even the ambiance you want to set, all controllable from your smartphone.

One of the most incredible AI integrations in your home can be virtual assistants. You hear voices from devices like Amazon Echo, Google Home, or Apple HomePod, and they are more than just responding to your commands to play music or read the news; they are now capable of managing your entire smart home ecosystem. Need to set reminders or manage your calendar? Just tell your assistant. Want to control your smart home devices without moving an inch? Ask your assistant to adjust the thermostat, turn off the lights, or lock the doors. With AI, these virtual helpers are learning to handle more complex tasks and provide real-time information that makes daily routines easier. It's like having a personal assistant who never takes a break and is always ready to help.

AI has transformed home safety measures with intelligent security systems. AI-enabled cameras are proactive, not reactive. They can now differentiate between normal and suspicious activities. Your smart security camera can distinguish between a car passing by and someone lurking suspiciously. This means better security and fewer false alarms—no more heart stopping moments when the cat sets off the motion detector.

E-Commerce and AI:

I'll bet the perfect item awaited your purchase the last time you logged into an online store. We are all familiar with that scenario. Some folks think it's listening to us talk, right? AI is a marketer's dream come true. It tracks your habits and suggests products based on the data you've already provided and agreed to provide in the future.

When you browse online stores, every click, every item you linger on, and every purchase you complete tells a story about your preferences. AI gathers all this to analyze and build a profile of your tastes, likes, and dislikes.

AI's role in e-commerce isn't just customer-facing. AI plays a crucial role in inventory management, analyzing sales data, and predicting future demand patterns. AI helps retailers understand which products will likely sell rapidly and which might need a promotional boost. This predictive capability allows for smarter inventory decisions, ensuring that popular items are well-stocked and less popular ones aren't over-ordered.

Have you ever noticed how the prices of products on some websites fluctuate almost daily? That's AI working behind the scenes using algorithms. AI analyzes factors of market demand, competitor pricing, and even time of day to adjust prices dynamically. For you, this might mean snagging a great deal on a product just when you're most likely to buy it. It means maintaining a steady sales flow by appealing to price-sensitive customers for the retailer. Please do not get me started on certain ticketing conglomerates and dynamic pricing or calling for a ride-share service after an event and their dynamic pricing. You'll see my workaround for ride-sharing later in this book.

Those friendly chatbots that pop up while you're shopping online. AI-powered chatbots are a game changer in customer service. They use natural language processing—a branch of AI that deals with the interaction between computers and humans—to understand and respond to your inquiries. Whatever you need: processing errors, tracking orders, finding a product, resolving issues, finding a solution, or possibly the right person to chat or talk to.

AI in Navigation, Transportation and Banking

Route Optimization: Imagine trying to get from point A to point B. Sounds simple, right? Throw in unpredictable traffic jams, road construction, or even rush hour, and suddenly, it's not so simple—AI steps in with route optimization. GPS technologies don't just show you the way; they analyze heaps of real-time traffic data to guide you on the quickest possible route. These systems assess the speed of traffic flow, look for accidents or road closures, and even consider historical traffic data to predict where delays might occur.

It's not just about avoiding traffic jams. AI navigation systems learn from your travel habits. The more you use it, the better it understands your preferences and tailors your route suggestions. It's like having a personal navigator who knows the roads better than anyone else and knows precisely how you like to travel on them. I love it when I get in my car, and the locations I travel to at that time of day are at the top of the suggested locations list.

Autonomous Vehicles: Not entirely yet. Some of us have been exposed to enhanced cruise control, which allows you to set the distance to follow the car in front of you and warns you if a vehicle is in your blind spot. Some AI GPS systems will give you the speed limit. Some enhanced "almost" self-driving cars change lanes when you put your blinker on. Autonomous driving is closer than ever.

Public Transport Management: AI manages everything from scheduling to real-time route adjustments, from buses and trains to subways. AI algorithms analyze passenger data to predict peak times and adjust transport schedules for maximum efficiency. This means more buses during rush hour and fewer late-night services when demand drops, optimizing energy use and reducing operational costs.

Ride-Sharing Algorithms: Ride-sharing apps like Uber and Lyft have become ubiquitous for many of us. When you request a ride, AI algorithms spring into action, matching with nearby drivers, much more sophisticated than who's closest. Algorithms analyze current traffic conditions, routes drivers are on, and even the rides they're currently completing. This optimizes your wait time and the driver's time on the road, reducing empty trips and unnecessary fuel consumption.

Anyone who has used rideshare programs knows all about pricing based on demand. It cost me less than $15 with a tip from my hotel in

San Francisco for the event I was attending. After the event, it was $45 to get back to my hotel. You can play the game of checking out all the competitors' prices. You will find it cheaper, but who wants to play that game, not me. I never plan on using ride-share to return from an event. I do one of two things. Well, it's a combination of the two. I take my time leaving the venue. I go to the designated ride-share pick-up spot. If there are many people, I start walking towards my destination and get a ride share about half a mile away. Or I pick out a place to go after the show. In this instance, as soon as the event ends, I move to that destination as quickly as possible. I have coffee or tea and possibly a piece of cake! When I am finished relaxing, the ride-share fare is much closer to my arrival fare.

Fraud Detection: First off, the superhero of smart banking (marketed as Innovative banking) fraud detection. Here's how it works: AI systems monitor your banking transactions in real-time, looking for patterns that deviate from your usual financial behaviors. Suppose all you usually use your card for is groceries and gas in your hometown, and there's a charge for a luxury watch on the other side of the globe. In that case, the AI system flags this transaction as suspicious and alerts you and the bank faster than you can imagine.

A few weeks ago, I looked at my phone. A text from my bank said to please call, stating there had been suspicious activity on my card. My card was shut down five minutes after speaking to the bank rep. I was told I could go to any branch to get a temporary card, and one would be at my house within five days. That has happened a few times. While traveling for work, I was in Houston and noticed a charge from a restaurant 450 miles away from Houston. My bank proactively removed the charge, immediately shut down the card, and sent a new one to my hotel the next day. I love AI fraud protection. And I still check each statement for errors.

Chapter Three

Creative Uses of AI

H ave you ever created a playlist that felt like a soundtrack to your life? From composing new melodies that could stir the soul to mixing tracks like a seasoned DJ, AI's role in the music industry is like having a high-tech maestro in your headphones.

AI in Music: Composition and Production

Algorithmic Composition: What if Beethoven or Mozart had a laptop? What type of symphonies would they compose with AI? AI algorithms in music composition analyze vast music databases, learning intricate melody, rhythm, and harmony patterns. That knowledge is used to generate stylistically similar but refreshingly original compositions.

Production Assistance: Music production is an art form of mixing sound. Mastering tracks is an art, not a science. AI software can help sound engineers and producers by adjusting levels, adding effects, or suggesting changes. This is about enhancing music, giving artists more tools for the creative process to express their musical visions, just like all the past advances in musical production and recording.

This tech wizardry is especially handy in live performances where AI systems can instantly mix and master music on the fly, adapting to the venue's acoustics or even the audience's live reactions. Imagine a concert where the music dynamically shifts to match the crowd's vibe, thanks to AI's real-time processing capabilities. It's like having an extra member of the band who's part psychic, part sound tech genius!

Personalization of Music Experience: Streaming services have changed how we listen to music, and AI has been the quiet powerhouse behind this revolution. The systems analyze your listening habits, picking up patterns like your favorite genres when you listen to certain songs and even what you skip. AI recommends music to fit your tastes.

AI in Film-Making and Editing: From indie filmmakers to blockbuster mega-capital studio productions, AI is changing how movies and TV are made.

Picture this: you've just wrapped up months of shooting a production. It's a high-energy, exciting time, and you are exhausted—AI steps in instead of spending hours reviewing footage, looking for that perfect shot. AI tools can now scan through the footage and find the perfect shots. These systems analyze each clip, considering factors like shot composition, actor expressions, and continuity to suggest or even automatically make edits that match the director's style. This isn't just about cutting down on the grunt work; it's about enhancing the creative process. Directors can experiment with different cuts or pacing, seeing in real time how these changes might play out without the risk of losing their original footage.

AI-driven visual effects (VFX). Filmmakers use AI to create breathtaking effects that blur the line between reality and CGI. Algorithms can create detailed, realistic backgrounds, changing the camera's perspective so that it's nearly impossible to detect where the set ends and the digital world begins.

These tools can animate characters interacting naturally with human actors, bringing fantastical creatures to life with unprecedented detail and realism. AI is making these stunning visuals more cost-effective, and smaller studios are now crafting visual spectacles that stand toe-to-toe with cinema giants, all thanks to AI leveling the playing field.

Switching gears, let's discuss AI in the writer's room. AI's ability to analyze scripts can be a game-changer for how stories are told on screen. By examining thousands of scripts and the performances of similar movies, AI can predict how audiences might react. It can suggest changes that make a scene more engaging or a character more relatable. Think of AI as a script advisor who's read every movie script ever written and watched how audiences reacted. This insight can be invaluable in tweaking scripts to better resonate with viewers and helping producers predict a film's box office potential before a single frame is shot.

I have been involved with Real-Time Rendering on sets. It is revolutionizing post-production, allowing filmmakers to render scenes in seconds. Real-time rendering creates visual effects so directors can quickly experiment and instantly see the impact. This can dramatically speed up post-production, allowing filmmakers to refine and tweak visuals long after the cameras have stopped rolling.

AI isn't just about technology; it's about unlocking new creative possibilities and making cinema's magic more dazzling and accessible than ever.

We've seen how AI isn't just changing the game; it's redefining the canvas of filmmaking and editing. AI's role in cinema is both transformative and expansive.

Chapter Four

Ethical AI Use and Considerations

I magine walking into a room where everyone knows your name—not because they know you, but because they've all peeked at your name tag. While it's fun to think of AI as the ultimate party trickster, dazzling us with personalized playlists and spot-on movie recommendations, there's a serious side to this: our privacy. It is essential to understand how these systems handle our personal data, the risks involved, and what it means to our private lives.

Privacy and AI:

Understanding Data Privacy: Privacy and AI involve how AI collects, uses, stores, and shares personal data. Data helps AI understand and predict your preferences, patterns, and behaviors, which must be handled carefully. AI systems need to be designed to respect privacy by securing the data they collect and ensuring it's used ethically. What are the risks?

For starters, there are data breaches, exposing sensitive information to folks who shouldn't see it. Then there is unauthorized surveillance—AI quietly watching or listening in without consent. These scenarios make anyone skeptical, especially if they already have a weak relationship with technology.

It's not all doom and gloom. There are superheroes in this story: privacy-enhancing technologies (PETs) are the tools designed to protect data as it's collected and processed, working behind the scenes to keep things safe. One is differential privacy, adding a bit of randomness to what AI analyzes. AI can learn patterns without pinpointing exact details. Another tool is federated learning, which means your data stays on your device instead of being sent over the internet. AI learns from many devices collectively without ever seeing the individual data points.

Regulations and Compliance: Enter regulations like the General Data Protection Regulation (GDPR) in the EU, which is like the rulebook for data privacy. They lay down the law on how data should be handled, giving individuals rights over their personal information. Companies that do not follow these rules face hefty fines, not to mention a severe loss of trust from users. Compliance isn't about avoiding penalties. It includes building systems that respect user privacy and promote transparency. It's about ensuring that AI serves us and not the other way around.

Bias in AI Causes, Consequences, and Mitigations. Bias is prejudice in favor of or against one thing.

Sources of Bias: AI systems learn from data; if the information they learn from is flawed and skewed, their outputs will be, too. If an AI system is trained on historical hiring data to screen job applicants, and that historical data reflects certain biases (favoring one demographic over another), AI will likely continue to perpetuate that bias. It's not about being malicious; it's simply working with what it's given. Another source is algorithmic bias, which occurs due to how algorithms are designed. The very logic that makes an AI function can lead to biased outcomes, especially if the algorithm's design doesn't account for a diverse set of scenarios or populations.

As mentioned, biased AI can lead to unfair hiring screening processes, where qualified candidates are overlooked simply because they don't fit the data patterns AI has learned. In credit scoring, biased AI might affect who gets approved for loans or who gets favorable interest rates, which can have long-term effects on individuals' financial health. In law enforcement, biased facial recognition technologies can misidentify individuals, leading to wrongful accusations. Strategies are employed to reduce bias. A key approach is diverse data sets. The need to include data from a wide range of sources and demographics gives AI a more holistic understanding of the world. Another strategy is conducting regular algorithmic audits, checking the AI's decision-making processes to ensure they aren't inadvertently biased. Inclusive design practices are critical, and diverse perspectives are needed in the AI development process from the get-go. By involving people from different backgrounds, one can ensure that the AI system considers a wide range of human experiences and is more likely to serve everyone fairly.

A notable case is a large tech company that noticed a trend where AI was favoring a particular demographic. After re-evaluating, the company expanded training data and adjusted the algorithm, leading to a more diverse selection that was much more equitable. They now conduct regular audits. Take the same example at financial institutions. They do regular audits of their AI processes for loan approvals to identify and correct biases for applicants.

Ethical AI Development: Best Practices

When baking a cake, you follow a recipe to ensure it comes out just right. But what if you're baking something a bit more complex, like an AI system? You'll need a really good set of recipes or ethical frameworks to make sure your AI doesn't just work efficiently but also responsibly. These frameworks are like grandma's tried-and-true baking guidelines, but for the digital age, ensuring that every slice of AI we create is just as fair as it is fabulous.

Consider them a collection of principles and guidelines that help developers keep their AI creations straight and narrow. Organizations like the IEEE (Institute of Electrical and Electronics Engineers) and entities like the European Union have developed comprehensive guidelines outlining how ethical AI is to be developed. These frameworks cover everything from ensuring AI respects user privacy and security to ensuring it's inclusive and accessible to everyone, regardless of background or ability. They're there to remind everyone in the AI kitchen—from data scientists to product managers—creating technology that impacts people's lives is a huge responsibility to be handled with care, consideration, and a hefty dose of ethical scrutiny.

Baking a good, ethical AI isn't a one-chef show. That's why involving diverse stakeholders in the AI development process is necessary. This means not just techies and data buffs but folks from all walks of life—ethicists, sociologists, potential users, and even representatives from marginalized communities. AI systems are designed to serve a diverse user base and can't be whipped up in a homogenous kitchen. They need a melting pot of ideas, concerns, and creative solutions.

Have you ever followed a recipe and ended up with something that looked nothing like the picture? The same goes for AI. Users need to understand how AI systems make decisions, especially when these decisions affect their lives. Whether it's a credit-scoring AI deciding your loan approval or a job screening AI evaluating your application, knowing how these decisions are made builds trust and accountability. Developers must create AI systems that explain their decisions in simple terms and document their processes clearly. This way, everyone from the end user to the regulators can understand the AI's decision-making recipe, ensuring it's fair, unbiased, and aligned with ethical standards.

You've probably heard the predictions that robots will steal all our jobs, leaving us to reminisce about the days when 'work' was a thing. AI is indeed reshaping the job landscape. It's a bit like a game of musical chairs—yes, some jobs might disappear, but new ones will pop up in their place.

First up, the tricky bit is job displacement. When it comes to routine, repetitive tasks, industries that rely heavily on such tasks, like manufacturing, data entry, and some aspects of customer service, are seeing more and more automation. AI is efficient. Let's face it: it's not great news for folks whose livelihoods depend on these roles. The transportation sector also looks like it's up for grabs, thanks to self-driving technology. Truck drivers, delivery folks, and even taxi drivers might need to shift gears career-wise as these autonomous solutions take the wheel.

On the brighter side—new job opportunities. AI isn't just about automation; it's also about augmentation. Think about roles in AI management, oversight, and ethical compliance. Someone needs to design, train, and manage AI systems. There's demand for folks who can bridge the gap between humans and machines—AI trainers who teach AI systems how to understand and interact with the world. Ethical AI advisors are on the rise. This transition will take time, just like previous Job Landscape transitions. It will not happen overnight. Lifelong learning comes into play just as AI continues to learn and adapt, so must we. Educational programs and training workshops to understand AI and its applications are crucial. From learning how to interact with AI systems to understanding data privacy and security, these programs prepare the workforce for a future where AI is as common as smartphones. The goal? To arm everyone from factory workers to CEOs with the skills needed to thrive in an AI-augmented workplace.

You're in your favorite coffee shop, and every move you make is monitored and analyzed by a network of cameras. It sounds like a Dystopian fiction movie. With AI-driven surveillance technologies, this scenario is close to being a reality. AI has the power to keep an eye on us like never before—from facial recognition to behavior prediction. While it sounds like Big Brother is watching a bit too closely, there's a flip side: these technologies significantly enhance public safety.

AI in surveillance isn't about mounting cameras on walls. There are algorithms to recognize your face in a crowd, understand your emotions, and even predict your next move. Behavior prediction technology analyzes movement patterns and predicts potential security threats based on deviations from these patterns.

The use of AI in surveillance raises privacy concerns. It can be unsettling knowing you can be constantly watched and analyzed. The risk of misuse in the wrong hands is on everyone's mind. Surveillance AI can become a tool for unwarranted monitoring, repression, or discrimination. Imagine a scenario where AI surveillance technology tracks and punishes specific groups of people unfairly. Not exactly the kind of future we want to sign up for, right?

We have the undeniable benefits of increased security and safety. Conversely, we have the fundamental right to privacy and personal freedom. Laws like GDPR in Europe provide a framework for protecting personal data, including data collected through surveillance. The legal landscape is still catching up to the rapid advancements in AI technology, and there's a patchwork of regulations globally, which can make consistent compliance and enforcement challenging.

Public perception of AI surveillance is mixed. Some people appreciate the enhanced security it brings, while others are deeply concerned about privacy and the potential for state overreach. Take a peek at the crime rates in areas where public police video surveillance is commonplace. There "seems to be" a significantly lower rate than in areas without. I do not have the answer; I am pointing to uses and a seemingly positive impact on security and safety.

The right balance between public safety and protecting individual privacy is a significant challenge that requires a collaborative approach involving policymakers, technology developers, civil society, and the public. A promising approach is privacy-preserving surveillance technologies, such as AI systems, that only store and analyze data when a potential threat is detected rather than continuously monitoring public spaces.

Ensuring the systems are used responsibly and with public consent, regular audits, and transparency reports on surveillance AI can also help hold authorities accountable, and these technologies are used ethically, giving the public more peace of mind.

In conclusion, as we step into the next chapter of AI's integration into our lives, we are navigating the delicate balance between innovation and ethics, especially regarding surveillance. By drawing clear ethical lines, open dialogue, and implementing robust safeguards, we can benefit from AI-driven surveillance and protect the values of privacy and personal freedom.

Chapter Five

AI Tools and
Hands-On Exercises

P rompts are a term you'll see as you educate yourself in Artificial
Intelligence. It's what you type or paste in the field for your request.
I started with straightforward prompts: edit this email to be... Then, I
became a little more detailed: "Create an email campaign that is engaging, fun, and entertaining, reaching out to the (whatever high school)
community regarding the marching band's Road to Rome, Italy trip to
march in the 1/1/2025 New Years Day Parade fundraiser carwash. *The
car wash is on X date. I need an email for the parents of the entire band
program every 2 weeks and a social media post weekly.* Something like the
below popped out:

NOTE: Below is an email campaign for the parents of band students
sample. Generative AI only goes so far. I heavily edited every single piece
of Generative AI. I needed to add our community tone and vibe to
every piece. As I write this, yet another element/software/App Google
extension is running the rounds for humanizing AI to replicate a more

human-sounding response; we will see how that turns out. When I did this in the 2023-2024 school year, I used timeframe and frequency suggestions and the output text as a frame of reference for the messaging.

Fundraising for the High School Band

Email 1 (Sent 8 weeks before the event)

Subject: Help Us Reach Rome! Support Our Marching Band Car Wash Fundraiser!

Dear Band Parents,

We are thrilled to announce our Road to Rome fundraiser car wash! On X date, our talented marching band will wash cars to raise funds for their exciting journey to Rome from 12/26/2024 to 1/3/2025.

Here's how you can support:

1. **Spread the Word:** Tell friends, family, and neighbors about the event.

2. **Volunteer:** We need parent volunteers to help with setup, manage the event, and cheer on our kids.

3. **Donate Supplies:** We need soap, sponges, towels, and refreshments for our hardworking students.

Stay tuned for more updates as we get closer to the date!

Thank you for your continuous support!

Best regards, [Your Name] High School Band Committee

Email 2 (Sent 6 weeks before the event)

Subject: Countdown to Our Car Wash Fundraiser! Can We Count on You?

Dear Band Parents,

Our Road to Rome car wash fundraiser is just six weeks away! Excitement is building, and we can't wait to see our community come together to support our amazing marching band.

How you can help:

- **Volunteer Sign-Up:** Click [here] to volunteer for a shift on the day of the car wash.

- **Supply Donations:** We still need a few more items. Check out our wishlist [here].

- **Spread the Word:** Share our event on social media and with your community. Every bit helps!

Let's make this fundraiser a roaring success!

Best regards, [Your Name] High School Band Committee

Something like this popped out for social media:

Week 3

Twitter Post:

Only 4 weeks until our car wash fundraiser! Come out and support the Marching Band on X date. #RoadToRomeCarWash #Band

Week 4

Facebook Post:

We need your help! Our car wash fundraiser is just two weeks away, and we still need volunteers and supplies. Click [here] to see how you can contribute. #RoadToRomeCarWash #Volunteer

Week 5

Instagram Post:

1 week to go! Are you ready to get your car washed by the best band in town? Join us next week and support our journey to Rome! #RoadToRomeCarWash #ParkviewBand

I did what it told me to do for car washes and our Casino Night/Silent Auction in the 2023-2024 school year.

Earlier, I mentioned the car washes raised just under $4,000. The Casino Night and the silent auction raised a net sum of $12,000. The return on time and energy invested in developing a marketing plan exceeded my expectations. I've spent thousands of man-hours creating less effective and engaging marketing campaigns. The execution was a different story. As is the case with volunteer organizations, the same 18% of the people *usually* do all the work/volunteering. To incentivize students' and parents' participation, we gave 90% of the funds raised to the students' band accounts to be used for band expenses such as yearly marching band fees, gloves, shoes, and, most importantly, the cost of the trip to Rome, Italy, New Year's Day Parade 2025. The remainder went to the band's general budget. That increased participation from 18%, or the usual suspects, to more parents and students. I imagine money seems to be a motivating factor in this instance.

Since then, I have uncovered a whole world of Facebook groups, YouTube videos, and other social media resources for using AI in business and anywhere else, and the applications are staggering. You can have your business work 24 hours a day gathering leads and marketing your goods and services for next to no money or spend as much as you like, all with no overtime.

Here are a few simple step-by-step exercises you can do today to introduce yourself to using AI and how easy it is. Some are more involved and require specialized equipment.

Using AI to Organize Your Photos

Have you ever found yourself scrolling endlessly through your phone's gallery, looking for that one perfect photo from last summer's beach trip? It's like finding a needle in a digital haystack. Enter AI, your new photo-organizing best friend. AI tools for managing digital photos are like efficient closet organizers. These tools can tag, sort, and categorize your images, turning a cluttered photo library into a neatly organized collection you can navigate with ease.

Tutorial on Photo Organization

Let's walk through setting up and using a popular AI-powered photo management tool like Google Photos or Apple Photos:

1. Getting Started: First, download the app and create an account if you don't have one already. Both platforms will offer to sync photos from your device automatically.

2. Initial Setup: Once your photos are uploaded, the AI begins working. It analyzes the images, identifying faces and other recognizable landmarks and objects. This process might take a while, especially if you have a lot of photos, but it's a one-time heavy lift.

3. Exploring Features: Dive into the features. Start by searching for a person, place, or thing in the search bar. Type "beach," and you'll see all your beach escapades, input a friend's name and every photo with their face pops up—like magic.

4. Creating Albums: You can manually create albums or let the AI suggest them based on events or locations. For instance, it might automatically generate an album titled "Weekend in New York" by grouping photos by date and geotags.

5. Face Tagging: For face recognition, most platforms will ask you to confirm if the faces it groups together are the same person. You can assign names, making future searches a breeze. Just type in "Mom" to pull up every photo from family gatherings, vacations, or random Tuesday dinners.

Why bother organizing your photos? It saves time. One of the most frustrating things about my phone is all the photos and how to find the one I am looking for to show someone. I end up looking at my phone, trying to find that one photo. Before too long, the conversation has stopped cause I'm looking at my phone, or the conversation has moved on, and the photo is useless. This is frustrating. Organized photos are a joy to explore. Instead of a chore, reminiscing becomes a pleasure as you rediscover forgotten moments. Plus, it's easier to share collections with friends or family. Instead of sending random photos, send an album titled "Christmas 2020," knowing it contains all the holiday cheer captured that year.

Beyond convenience, there's something more profound about looking back at well-organized memories. It's about preserving your life's story in a way that's accessible and meaningful. Each photo tells a part of your story, and organizing them helps ensure these stories aren't lost in the digital void.

Privacy Considerations

Now, while it's great to have AI sort through your digital memories, it's important to consider privacy. Please do not just assume that the evil Big Brother is using/selling all your data. These AI tools often operate in the cloud, which means your photos are analyzed on remote servers. *Here's how to keep your precious memories safe* while benefiting from AI organization:

Read the Privacy Policies. I know, I know, I know. Privacy policies are boring and filled with lawyer speak. However, reading them is the only way to know what data the service collects and how it's used. Ensure you're comfortable with their terms before uploading your photos.

Use Trusted Services: Choose reputable providers like Google, Apple, or Amazon, with clear privacy policies and security measures.

Check Sharing Settings: Make sure you understand the sharing settings. Set albums to private or share them only with specific people.

Local Backup: Consider keeping a local backup of your photos. I have a 2TB external hard drive that I set to back up my laptop when I Plug it in. I set a reminder to plug it in every two weeks. It is the size of a ½" thick business card. External hard drives or personal cloud storage devices can store your images without the need for third-party services.

Organizing your photos with AI isn't just about decluttering your digital space; it's about securing and cherishing your personal history in the digital age. With these tools, your photo library transforms from a chaotic collection into a curated gallery, where every memory is preserved and easily accessible, just a few clicks away. So why wait? Let AI help you organize your digital memories and rediscover the joy of reliving those precious moments.

Simple AI Projects for Home Automation

I have done some of these home automation projects. I enjoy the ease of use after it is set up. A word of caution: Plan to allow for double the amount of time you think it will take. It will get easier the more frequently you automate.

Automating your Home: Install a Smart Thermostat

You can use any smart thermostat.

Step 1: Gather Tools and Materials

Ensure you have the thermostat unit, base plate, screws, wire labels, and installation guide.

Tools: Screwdriver (Phillips and flathead), drill (if needed), level, smartphone or tablet.

Have the Smart Thermostat installation guide and user manual handy.

Step 2: Turn Off Power

Safety First: Turn off the power to your HVAC system at the circuit breaker to avoid electrical shock.

Verify: Confirm the power is off by adjusting your current thermostat. If the system doesn't respond, the power is off.

Step 3: Remove the Old Thermostat

Take a Photo: Before removing any wires, take a photo of the existing wiring setup for reference.

Use the provided wire labels to mark each wire according to its terminal designation (e.g., R, W, Y, G, C).

Carefully disconnect the wires from the old thermostat.

Unscrew and remove the base plate of the old thermostat from the wall.

Step 4: Install the Smart Thermostat Base

Mount the Base: Position the Smart Thermostat base on the wall. Use a level to ensure it's straight.

Mark the locations of the screw holes if you need to drill new ones.

Drill holes if necessary and insert wall anchors.

Screw the Smart Thermostat base into the wall securely.

Step 5: Connect the Wires

Reference Photo: Use your earlier photo and the wire labels to guide you.

Connect each wire to the corresponding terminal on the Smart base plate. Press the button and insert the wires to fasten them securely.

Common Wire (C-Wire): If your setup has a C-wire, connect it to the C terminal. If not, Smart thermostats can often work without it, but if needed, use the power adapter kit or consult an HVAC professional.

Step 6: Attach the Smart Display

Attach the Smart Thermostat display to the base plate. It should snap into place easily.

Step 7: Turn On Power

Go back to the circuit breaker and turn the power back on for your HVAC system.

Step 8: Configure the Thermostat

The Smart Thermostat will power up. Follow the on-screen instructions to set up your thermostat. This includes selecting your language, connecting to Wi-Fi, and entering basic home and HVAC system information.

Use the thermostat's interface to connect to your home Wi-Fi network.

Step 9: Download the Smart App

Download the Smart app from the App Store or Google Play Store.

If you don't already have one, create one using the Smart app.

To add your new thermostat, follow the app's instructions. You will need to enter a code displayed on the thermostat.

Step 10: Customize Settings

Set your preferred temperature schedules.

Enable features like Home/Away Assist, Eco Temperatures, and Learning Mode.

Explore Settings: Customize other settings as per your preference through the Smart app.

Step 11: Test the System

Ensure the thermostat can control your heating and cooling system as expected.

Make any necessary adjustments to the settings and ensure the system responds correctly.

Additional Tips:

Check for any firmware updates for your thermostat and install them via the app.

Enable learning algorithms if you are so trusting (tee hehe) for energy-saving features like auto-away, learning algorithms, and scheduled temperature adjustments.

Support: Consult the Smart Thermostat user manual or online support if you encounter any issues during installation.

By following these steps, you can successfully set up your Smart Thermostat and enjoy a more comfortable and energy-efficient home.

Install a Smart Light

including connecting it to Siri, Alexa, and Google Home:

Step 1: Setting Up the Smart Light

Unbox Your Smart Light:

Remove the smart light bulb from its packaging.

Screw the smart light bulb into a light socket or fixture.

Turn on the Light:

Ensure the light switch controlling the socket is in the "on" position.

Step 2: Connecting to Wi-Fi

Download the app specified by the smart light manufacturer (e.g. , Philips Hue, TP-Link Kasa).

Open the app and follow the instructions to create an account if you don't already have one.

Follow the in-app instructions to add the new smart light to your account. This usually involves selecting "Add Device" or a similar option.

Select your Wi-Fi network and enter the password when prompted to connect the smart light to your home Wi-Fi network.

Step 3: Connecting to Siri (Apple HomeKit)

Open the Apple Home app on your iPhone or iPad.

Tap the "+" button to add a new accessory.

Scan the HomeKit setup code found on the smart light or in its packaging.

Follow the on-screen instructions to assign the light to a room and give it a name.

Use Siri to control the light by saying, "Hey Siri, turn on the [Light Name]."

Step 4: Connecting to Amazon Alexa

Open the Amazon Alexa app on your smartphone.

Tap on "Devices" at the bottom right, then tap the "+" icon and select "Add Device."

Choose the type of smart light you're adding from the list.

Follow the instructions to discover and connect your smart light.

You can use Alexa to control the light by saying, "Alexa, turn on the [Light Name]."

Step 5: Connecting to Google Home

Open the Google Home app on your smartphone.

Tap the "+" icon at the top left, then select "Set up device."

Select "Works with Google" and choose the manufacturer of your smart light.

Follow the prompts to link your smart light account with Google Home.

Assign the light to a specific room in your home.

You can use Google Assistant to control the light by saying, "Hey Google, turn on the [Light Name]."

Tips for Troubleshooting

Ensure Wi-Fi is 2.4 GHz: Many smart lights only support 2.4 GHz Wi-Fi networks.

If the connection fails, try restarting your router, smartphone, and smart light.

Ensure all related apps are up-to-date.

⌐heul Permissions Make sure the apps have the necessary permissions to access your device's location and network.

With this guide, your smart light should be up and running, fully integrated with Siri, Alexa, or Google Home. Enjoy the convenience of controlling your lighting with just your voice!

Install a Security Camera

Including connecting it to Siri, Alexa, and Google Home:

Step-by-Step Guide to Setting Up a Ring or Similar Security Camera System

Step 1: Unboxing and Initial Setup

Remove the camera, power adapter/battery, mounting hardware, and any other accessories from the box.

Plug the camera into a power source or insert the battery if it's battery-operated. Ensure it is fully charged if required.

Download the Ring app (or the app specified by your camera's manufacturer) from the App Store (iOS) or Google Play Store (Android).

Create an Account: Open the app and follow the instructions to create a new account or log in if you already have one.

Step 2: Setting Up the Security Camera

Select "Set Up a Device" in the app and choose "Security Cameras" or the appropriate device category.

To connect your camera to your Wi-Fi network, follow the step-by-step instructions provided in the app. You may need to scan a QR code on the camera.

Decide on the location of your camera. Mount it using the provided hardware. Ensure it has a good Wi-Fi signal and covers the desired area. Use the app to view the camera feed and adjust the angle if necessary. Ensure the camera is capturing the desired area.

Step 3: Connecting to Siri (Apple HomeKit)

Open the Apple Home app on your iPhone or iPad.

Tap the "+" button to add a new accessory.

Scan the HomeKit setup code on the camera or in its packaging (if the camera supports it).

Follow the on-screen instructions to assign the camera to a room and name it.

Use Siri to view the camera feed by saying, "Hey Siri, show me the [Camera Name]."

Step 4: Connecting to Amazon Alexa

Open the Amazon Alexa app on your smartphone.

Go to the "Skills & Games" section, search for the camera manufacturer's skill (e.g., Ring), and enable it.

Log in with your camera account credentials to link your camera account with Alexa.

Tap "Devices" at the bottom right, then tap the "+" icon and select "Add Device" to discover your camera.

Use Alexa to view the camera feed by saying, "Alexa, show me the [Camera Name]."

Connecting to Google Home:

Open the Google Home app on your smartphone.

Tap the "+" icon at the top left, then select "Set up device" and choose "Works with Google."

Select the camera manufacturer (e.g., Ring) from the list.

Follow the prompts to link your camera account with Google Home.

Assign the camera to a specific room in your home.

You can use Google Assistant to view the camera feed by saying, "Hey, Google, show me the [Camera Name]."

Tips for Troubleshooting

Place the camera within range of a strong Wi-Fi signal to avoid connectivity issues.

If you encounter issues, try restarting your router, smartphone, and camera.

Ensure all related apps are up-to-date.

Make sure the apps have the necessary permissions to access your device's location, camera, and network.

With this guide, your security camera should be set up and integrated with Siri, Alexa, or Google Home, providing comprehensive home security and convenience.

Safety and Security Tips

As you get your home automation projects up and running, keeping safety and security in mind is crucial. Always use products from reputable brands that support secure wireless standards. Regularly update your devices to protect against vulnerabilities, and use strong, unique passwords for any related accounts. For devices like smart thermostats or locks, consider additional layers of security such as two-factor authentication, ensuring that even if a password is compromised, your home's critical systems remain protected.

Diving into home automation enhances your living space and adds magic to your daily routines. Whether you're adjusting the lighting for the perfect ambiance or coming home to the perfect temperature, each project adds convenience and efficiency, ultimately creating a home that's not just smart but also more aligned with your lifestyle.

Using AI for Health and Fitness Goals

A personal coach who never sleeps, eats, or takes a break could enhance your fitness journey. It's revolutionizing how we approach our health and fitness goals. Whether you're trying to shed a few pounds, a busy professional looking to optimize your limited workout time, or someone who needs to keep a close eye on your heart rate, glucose levels, and sleep patterns. Fitness apps and wearables equipped with AI are like having a personal trainer and health expert rolled into one, always ready to offer tailored advice and insights based on your unique data.

AI in Personal Health and Fitness

How does AI make health transformations possible? Wearable devices like Fitbit or Apple Watch monitor everything from your heart rate and steps to your sleep patterns and stress levels. These devices use AI to analyze the data they collect, providing insights to help you optimize your health and fitness routines. Tracking your sleep patterns, AI can determine the best times for you to go to bed and wake up, ensuring optimal rest. By monitoring your heart rate during different exercises, AI suggests which workouts are most effective for your fitness goals and current health.

It's not just about collecting data; it's about making sense and providing beneficial actions. Algorithms detect trends and patterns in your health data that would be difficult to spot. If you're logging your meals and physical activities, AI will help you understand how your food intake affects your workout or weight loss. It's like having a dietitian and a personal trainer discussing the best strategies to help you succeed on your wrist or phone.

Starting with AI-enhanced fitness tools may seem daunting, but they are relatively straightforward. Most health and fitness apps today have user-friendly interfaces that guide you through setting up your profile and goals. Here's how you can get started:

Choose any app; I am sure your phone has a default Health app. Find the search function on your phone and search Health on Fitness, then

1. Define Your Goals: Are you looking to lose weight, build muscle, or improve your overall health? Set clear, achievable goals. Remember, AI works best when it has specific targets to aim for.

2. Input Your Data: Enter as much information as possible—your age, weight, height, dietary restrictions, typical sleep hours, and any health issues. The more data AI has, the more accurately it can tailor its advice. TIP: I always add a number of days to any app or software requesting my date of birth.

3. Integrate Other Devices: If you have wearable devices like a fitness band or a smartwatch, ensure they're synced with your health app. This integration allows AI to pull in data automatically, giving it a comprehensive view of your health.

4. Start Tracking: As you begin your fitness regimen, keep logging your activities and meals. This ongoing data feeds the AI, enabling it to refine its suggestions and make adjustments to your plan as needed.

Once you're all set up, AI tools continuously analyze your input. It's not just about counting steps or calories; it's about understanding how different aspects of lifestyle contribute to overall health. AI might suggest taking a rest day if stress levels are high or recommend a higher protein intake if you're ramping up your strength training. Over time, AI learns about you and suggests increasingly personalized, more practical advice.

Privacy and Data Management

Now, while it's exciting to have AI as your health ally, it's crucial to consider the privacy of your health data. These tips can help you manage your data securely:

- Read Privacy Policies: Before downloading any app, read its privacy policy to understand how your data will be used and protected.

- Use Secure Apps: Depending on your location, opt for apps from reputable developers that comply with health data regulations such as HIPAA or GDPR.

- Control Data Sharing: Be cautious about which apps you allow to share your health data. Regularly review app permissions to ensure your data isn't being shared more widely than you'd like.

- Regular Updates: Keep your apps and devices updated to protect against security vulnerabilities.

You can enjoy the benefits of AI-driven health and fitness tools while keeping your sensitive data safe and secure. Whether you're a newbie or a seasoned athlete, AI has something to offer and provides insights and suggestions just for you, making your path to health and fitness as efficient and enjoyable as possible. Why not let AI take the guesswork out of your health and fitness routine?

AI Tools for Everyday Problem Solving

Between juggling work, maintaining the home, and trying to have some semblance of a social life, we are easily overwhelmed. AI isn't just for tech whizzes and big corporations, but something that can be right at home in your daily routine, helping you tackle everything from mundane tasks like scheduling to keeping your finances in check. Let's see how you can begin to have AI simplify your everyday life, making room for more of what you love to do.

First, consider the little things that consume your time or cause stress. It could be keeping up with your endless to-do list, managing your budget after a holiday splurge, or planning meals while trying to stay healthy. These might seem like minor issues, but they add up, taking away from your peace of mind and free time. The good news? There's likely an AI tool ready to take these burdens off your shoulders.

For instance, if scheduling is your nemesis, AI can help you efficiently manage your calendar, suggesting the best meeting times based on your work habits and existing commitments. Or budget tracking, which has you tangled up in spreadsheets and receipts. AI financial assistants can analyze your spending patterns, help you set budgets, and save money. When it comes to meal planning, imagine an AI kitchen assistant who suggests recipes based on what's in your fridge, aligns with your dietary preferences, and even helps you shop for groceries online. There are plenty of other apps than the ones I mentioned. You can do a Google search for others.

Budgeting / Scheduling

Let's explore some AI tools that can help solve these everyday challenges. For scheduling, tools like Reclaim.AI offer automated scheduling assistants that sync with your calendar. It can handle appointment requests, reschedule meetings, and ensure you never double-book yourself. For budget tracking, apps like Mint (currently under Credit Karma) or YNAB (You Need A Budget has a trial offer before purchase) use AI to track your spending and provide real-time insights, offering personalized tips to improve your savings.

Meal-planning apps

Mealime (free app at printing) or PlateJoy (free online trial) use AI to create customized meal plans based on your dietary preferences and time constraints. They even generate shopping lists that integrate directly with online grocers. These tools learn from your feedback, adjusting over time to suit your taste and nutritional needs better.

Educational AI Tools

If you are stuck in a learning rut or want to pick up a new skill but can't find the right resources or the time, AI-powered educational tools aren't typical classroom tools. They're innovative platforms that adapt to your learning style, making education a truly tailored experience. Imagine a tool that teaches and learns about you and from you, shaping courses and content to fit what you need when you need it.

Language learning apps like Duolingo (free with ads, add free for a price) and platforms like Khan Academy (no cost at the time of publishing this book) offer courses on a wide array of subjects. These platforms use algorithms to provide personalized learning experiences. Content that adjusts based on your interaction patterns and the mastery of the material. For instance, if you're acing your Spanish vocabulary but can't seem to get the hang of grammar, the AI will adjust lessons to focus more on grammar rules, providing additional exercises to help you improve.

Coursera (free and fee-based) and Udacity (subscription-based) bring AI into professional development with courses designed to boost your career skills in areas like data science, programming, and even artificial intelligence. The platforms analyze learning progress and tailor the curriculum to teach at your pace while still facing enough challenges to keep you engaged and moving forward.

Benefits of AI in Education

The beauty of using AI is in its flexibility and efficiency. Personalized learning paths created by AI mean you no longer have to learn topics you already know or skip crucial information you need. AI identifies strengths and weaknesses to customize the content accordingly, ensuring time spent learning is always productive.

AI tools include features such as virtual tutors, interactive quizzes, and games to make learning more engaging. Unlike traditional one-size-fits-all educational environments, AI-enhanced learning gives everyone a way to learn that is best suited to them, making education inclusive and more effective.

Say you want to learn a new language; apps like Duolingo use AI to guide you through learning with exercises tailored to your progress and reminders sent based on your study habits. For coding, platforms like Codecademy (basic free, other levels monthly fee) or GitHub's Copilot (free, $4 a month & $21 a month with a free trial) offer interactive coding environments where AI helps debug your code, suggest improvements, and even predict what you might want to type next.

Self-educating has never been easier thanks to LinkedIn Learning and Google AI, which offer courses on topics from marketing to machine learning, all curated based on your career interests and skills. These platforms track your progress and suggest new courses to ensure you're always prepared for whatever your career throws at you.

Incorporating AI learning tools into your daily routine can be a game-changer, especially when juggling a busy schedule. Set aside as little as fifteen minutes daily to engage with an AI learning app; it's like having a mini classroom in your pocket, ready whenever you are. Over time, these moments add up, significantly improving your knowledge and skills without overwhelming your day.

Use the platforms' built-in tracking and reminder systems to keep momentum. They'll help keep you accountable and ensure you're consistently building on what you've learned. Remember, continuous learning is critical to personal and professional growth, and with AI educational tools, there's no limit to what you can learn or how far you can go.

Start today. Pick a tool that matches your interests, set a small daily learning goal, and watch as AI helps you grow in ways you never thought possible. Whether picking up a new hobby, mastering a professional skill, or satisfying your curiosity, AI-powered educational tools are your allies on this exciting learning adventure. With each session tailored to your needs, learning becomes not just a task but a journey of discovery and improvement.

Advanced DIY AI Project – Build a Smart Mirror

This is an advanced project and will require learning something if not something's. If you do not know what something is in this project, Google it like all the kids are doing or search YouTube. If you search for what you don't know verses being satisfied with I do not know that's almost all the battle. It's only a search away and if you hate google use ∩ˌ₁ ₁₁ ₁ ₁

These are abridged instructions. Be sure to research each step on your own. There are many action items not listed in the 10,000 foot overview of building a smart mirror.

Building a Smart Mirror

Ever fantasized about a mirror that doesn't just reflect but interacts? Welcome to the concept of the smart mirror—a delightful blend of fairy tale magic and modern technology. This isn't just any mirror; it's like your morning newspaper, weather forecaster, and notification center, all rolled into one sleek reflective surface. Imagine getting ready in the morning and having a mirror display the time, weather updates, news headlines, and personal reminders like birthday reminders or meeting notifications. It's like having a personal assistant in your bathroom, only cool-er!

A smart mirror displays various information on its surface, effectively combining your reflection with data from the internet, all in real time. It utilizes a semi-transparent mirror hidden behind a display device (like a monitor or TV screen). When the display shows white content, it appears as if it's floating on the mirror's surface—a truly futuristic effect! This setup is not just for tech-savvy or gadget enthusiasts; it's for anyone who loves a bit of efficiency and magic sprinkled throughout their day.

I advise you to at least look at this website https://magicmirror.buil ders/

There is a great video introducing a smart mirror. When I showed it to my wife, she said, "I want a smart mirror."

What you will need before diving into building your own smart mirror:

Two-Way Mirror: A special mirror that is reflective on one side and transparent on the other, allowing the display behind it to be seen only when activated.

Display: Behind the two-way mirror, a monitor or an old TV can serve as the display. The size depends on how large you want your smart mirror to be.

Raspberry Pi: This small but powerful computer will run your smart mirror software. It's the brain of your operation.

SD Card: This is used to install the operating system and smart mirror software on the Raspberry Pi. [this is an opportunity to get out of your comfort zone of not knowing. If you do not know what a Raspberry Pi is google it]

HDMI Cable: To connect your Raspberry Pi to your monitor or TV.

Frame: To house your monitor and the two-way mirror, giving your smart mirror a finished look.

Relevant Software: MagicMirror[2] is a popular open-source software many DIYers use to run their smart mirrors. It's customizable with different modules.

Assembly Instructions

1. Prepare the Raspberry Pi: First, install an operating system (like Raspbian) on the SD card. Then, connect the Raspberry Pi to a monitor using your HDMI cable and boot it up. (If you do not know what a Raspberry Pi is google it)

2. Install Smart Mirror Software: Download and install MagicMirror[2] or any other smart mirror software onto the Raspberry Pi. This software will manage what's displayed on your smart mirror.

3. Configure the Display Module: Adjust the settings according to what information you want to be displayed. Choose from modules like weather, news feed, calendar, etc. Customizing your smart mirror's display allows you to tailor it to your daily needs.

4. Assemble the Frame and Mirror: Place the two-way mirror in the frame. Ensure that the reflective side faces out. Behind this, mount your display (monitor or TV), aligning it so that the display area matches the visible area of the mirror.

5. Final Setup: Connect the display to the Raspberry Pi using the HDMI cable. Power up the Raspberry Pi and tweak the display settings until the software's output aligns perfectly with the portion of the mirror you want it to show through.

6. Mounting: Secure the entire setup where you want your smart

mirror—usually in the bathroom or bedroom. Make sure it's near a power source and secure on the wall.

Voila! You've just created a gadget that you can use to trim unwanted facial hair or if you need an umbrella for the day. This project adds a touch of futuristic luxury to your daily routine and gets you hands-on with some of the most extraordinary tech.

By tackling this smart mirror project, you've entered a world where everyday objects are more interactive, helpful, and fun. Each component you assemble plays a part in bringing a dash of digital magic right into your daily reflection session. Sure, it's a bit more complex than other DIY projects, but the payoff is enormous—a mirror that shows your reflection and helpful information tailored just for you. So go ahead and give it a try. Who knows what other everyday items you might decide to smarten up next?

As we close this chapter on AI tools and hands-on projects, reflect on how these applications simplify tasks and add joy and discovery to everyday interactions. Each project is a step towards integrating more intuitive technology into our lives, making the day-to-day not just more accessible but also a lot more interesting. Looking ahead, we'll explore how these technologies shape industries and what that means for future innovations.

Make a Difference with Your Review - Unlock the Power of Generosity

"No one has ever become poor by giving." – Anne Frank

Thank you so much for diving into ***AI for Beginners: Skeptics Guide Automate Tasks, Streamline Your Life & Expand Your Earnings with Fun, Easy Exercises Anyone Can Do – NO TECH SKILLS Needed!*** I hope this book has helped you see AI can simplify life and even help you earn more.

Now, I need *your* help. Just like you've taken the time to explore new ideas, you can make a big impact by sharing your experience with others. Your honest review could be the key to helping someone else take their first step into the world of AI. Pretty awesome, right?

Here's why your review matters. **You're Helping Others**. By sharing what you think, you're giving someone else the nudge they need to start their own journey with AI, just like you did. **AI might seem like something for tech experts,** but with your feedback, we can show people that *anyone* can use it—no tech skills required!

Please take a minute, share your thoughts, and let others know about this book. It doesn't have to be fancy—just your honest opinion is perfect. Your words might inspire someone to read this.

How to Leave a Review: Click the QR code -

Or click/follow this link - https://www.amazon.com/review/review-your-purchases/error?asin=BOOKASINB0DJB2CY6K

Tell your story about how this book has made a difference for you!

Thanks again for being a part of this exciting journey. Your review is a simple yet powerful way to pay it forward.

Together, we can make a difference!

Warmly,

Tony Williams

Chapter Six

AI for Career Advancement

The world of Artificial Intelligence is a high-speed train that's already left the station. This chapter is about transforming you into the conductor of your AI journey right in your career. Whether you're the office newbie or the seasoned pro, integrating AI into your professional life doesn't just add a shiny new skill to your resume—it propels you forward in a world where digital savvy isn't just excellent to have. It's almost necessary. Let's see if we can entice AI into your career co-pilot.

There's always a learning curve. How well you navigate those inevitable bumps—the "interruptions to lifelong learning"—determines your success in self-education. What are these interruptions? They show up as frustration, confusion, doubt, or even that nagging voice telling you, "I can't" or "I'll never change."

The key isn't in trying to silence these voices or make them disappear; instead, recognize them for what they are. They've been with you for a long time, and it'll take time for their grip to loosen. But as you continue, you'll find they impact you less and less. Stay at your pace, and you'll grow more adept at quieting their influence.

AI Skills for the Non-Techie Professional

Navigating the AI landscape can feel like trying to order coffee in a foreign language. What do you need, and what's just noise? Understanding what AI skills are relevant to your industry can dramatically change your professional game. It's not about coding (unless you want it to be); it's about understanding the capabilities of AI and how they can solve real problems in your field. For instance, in marketing, grasping data analytics tools can help you understand consumer behavior more deeply. Knowing how chatbots and automated responses work in customer service can streamline processes and improve customer satisfaction.

Think of AI skills as tools in a toolbox—some you'll use every day, others on rare occasions, but all are worth knowing about. Start by identifying pain points in your job or industry that AI could alleviate. Is data overload a constant issue? Look into data visualization tools. Does customer query response time need improvement? Explore AI-driven chat support systems. It's about finding the right tool for the right job.

How do you get AI know-how without going back for another degree? The internet is teeming with resources designed to make AI available and approachable to everyone. Coursera.org and Udemy.com offer courses tailored for non-techies, covering everything from basic AI concepts to specific applications like AI for project management or digital marketing. For those who prefer a more structured approach, coding boot camps like GeneralAssembly.ly often include AI fundamentals in their curriculum, even for those not pursuing a developer track.

Books are a fantastic resource. Titles like "AI For Everyone" by Andrew Ng break down complex ideas into digestible bits. Podcasts, YouTube channels, and even AI-focused blogs can provide ongoing learning. The goal isn't to become a master overnight but to build a solid foundation and grow from there. Writing this book is part of my ongoing education. I have visited and worked with some of the same tools I am writing about and have spent a ton of time on the IBM platform SkillsBuild.

You've got _some_ AI knowledge—now what? Start small. Implement AI tools that can automate tedious tasks. For example, if you're drowning in emails, try an email sorting tool that uses AI to prioritize your inbox. If project deadlines are constantly stressful, project management software with AI can optimize your schedules and predict potential holdups.

Another practical tip: use AI to enhance your presentations. Tools like Canva.com and Prezi.com now offer AI-driven design suggestions, making your slides prettier and more effective by aligning with best design practices.

As we grow more comfortable with AI, don't keep it to yourself—make sure it's visible on your resume, LinkedIn profile, and interviews. Specific AI skills, backed by examples of how you've used them to achieve results, can set you apart in the job market. For instance, if you used an AI tool to reduce project completion times by 30%, that's a compelling bullet point that catches anyone's eye!

In interviews, be ready to discuss what you've done with AI and how you see it impacting your role and industry in the future. Your proactive approach to learning and applying AI speaks volumes about your drive and adaptability—qualities that may be lacking in today's fast-paced work environment. More is not always better, and adaptability is always best.

Interactive Element: AI Skills Assessment Quiz

To help you identify which AI skills might best boost your career, here's a quick quiz to get you thinking about where you could start:

- Do you find that you might overwhelming?

- Have you ever felt stuck doing repetitive tasks?

- Could AI help in managing schedules and deadlines?

- Are you interested in using AI to enhance customer interaction?

Each 'Yes' is a potential starting point for your AI skill development, guiding you toward areas where AI can significantly impact your daily work and career growth.

Embracing AI doesn't demand tech expertise—it only asks for curiosity, basic know-how, and, most importantly, patience. Patience is essential, especially for skeptics who constantly wrestle with their thoughts and that voice in their heads.

We all have that voice. It's always there, narrating everything. Here's an example I often use in presentations: when I mention the voice, people ask, "What voice?"

Then, I stop talking. Silence. The room becomes uncomfortable, and people grow uneasy. And then I say, "That voice—the one that just wondered why I stopped talking or thought you knew why or started planning what's for dinner. That voice talks you into, out of, and around things that might push you into an uncomfortable situation. All *your inner* voice wants is comfort".

With these tools and tips, you *could* be on your way to making AI a valuable ally in your career advancement and to a future where you and AI collaborate to achieve more than you ever thought possible. However, it would be best if you learned how to self-educate. To do that, you may want to identify what your voice says about you and where you relinquish your power and your say to that voice.

Incorporating AI into Your Business or Startup

Ever wished you had a magic wand to wave over your business operations to make everything run smoothly and smartly? AI is real and ready to transform your businesses or startups from the inside out. Running a bustling bakery or a tech startup, integrating AI into your business processes is a smart way to utilize its power.

Running a business involves juggling many balls—inventory, customer relationships, logistics—you name it! Imagine if AI could keep a few of those balls in the air for you. In inventory management, AI can predict stock needs based on historical sales data, seasonal trends, and even current market analysis. Say goodbye to overstocking (and the dreaded markdowns that follow) or, worse, running out of stock just when demand spikes. Similarly, in customer relationship management (CRM), AI analyzes customer interactions and feedback and helps you understand what your customers want, providing better service and, ultimately, a loyal customer base. Regarding logistics, AI can optimize delivery routes in real-time, considering traffic, weather, and vehicle load, ensuring products get to where they need to be quickly and cost-effectively.

AI is your ultra-efficient, never-tired business consultant who's always on call. By automating these essential, time-consuming tasks, AI frees up time to focus on what matters: growth and innovation. The insights AI provides help you make smarter business decisions, reducing guesswork and costly mistakes.

AI-driven Decision Making

Let's dive deeper into decision-making. Businesses are filled with decision-making, from the strategic to the mundane. AI sifts through massive amounts of data and provides insights that might not be obvious even to the most experienced entrepreneurs. For example, by analyzing customer purchase patterns, AI can help you identify emerging trends or suggest new products that could be big hits. It can also accurately forecast sales, helping you confidently plan for the future.

AI's superpower lies in its ability to provide insights and predict outcomes. This predictive power can be a game-changer in areas like market analysis, financial planning, and risk management. By understanding potential future scenarios, you can make decisions—not just reactive decisions but proactive decisions, positioning your business to capitalize on opportunities and avoid pitfalls.

Case Studies of AI in Small Businesses

Consider the story of a small online boutique that used AI to personalize shopping experiences. By implementing an AI algorithm that analyzed each visitor's browsing behavior, the boutique could suggest products that customers were more likely to purchase, causing a 30% increase in sales and a higher customer return rate.

An example of a local coffee shop that used AI to manage its supply chain. By predicting peak times and customer preferences, the coffee shop was able to optimize its inventory and staffing, reducing waste and improving customer service.

Overcoming Challenges

Of course, integrating AI into your business isn't without its challenges. Cost can be a barrier, especially for startups and small businesses. The cost of AI technology is decreasing as it becomes more widespread. The return on investment, in terms of both time and money saved, often outweighs the initial costs. Complexity can also be daunting. The key is to start small. Choose one area of your business that could benefit most from AI and pilot a project, making the process less overwhelming and allowing you to see tangible results quickly, build momentum, and buy-in for further AI integration.

Another common hurdle is resistance to change, which can be incredibly challenging in businesses with established ways of doing things. Here, communication is crucial. Highlight how AI can make employees' jobs easier and more productive rather than simply replacing human roles. Offering training and upskilling opportunities can also help ease the transition, turning potential skeptics into AI advocates.

Incorporating AI into your business or startup is less about jumping on the bandwagon and more about strategically leveraging technology to enhance your operations, make informed decisions, and stay competitive in a rapidly evolving marketplace. Whether it's through improving efficiency, gaining insights, or driving innovation, AI has the potential to transform the way you do business fundamentally. So why not let AI be your partner in navigating the complex business landscape? The future isn't just about keeping up; it's about leading the way, and with AI, you're well-equipped to set the pace.

AI in Healthcare: Opportunities for Professionals

Imagine walking into a hospital where your diagnosis and treatment are informed by a tool so sharp it consistently outpaces even the Smartest human minds in spotting nuances in medical data. This isn't a snippet from a futuristic novel; it's the reality of today's healthcare landscape transformed by Artificial Intelligence. From the examination room to the operating table, AI is reshaping how care is delivered, making it more precise, personalized, and preemptive. Let's unwrap these advancements and see how they're making waves in the medical field.

AI tools are not just another gadget in the doctor's bag—they are revolutionary. Take imaging diagnostics, for example. AI algorithms trained on thousands, sometimes millions, of images can detect abnormalities such as tumors, fractures, or blockages with astonishing accuracy. These tools are like having an ultra-detailed detective scan every pixel of an MRI or X-ray, often catching early signs of diseases that even experienced radiologists might miss. Then there's predictive analytics, where AI comes into play by crunching vast amounts of medical data to predict health risks. It can analyze everything from genetic information to lifestyle choices, giving healthcare providers a heads-up on potential health issues before they turn into serious problems. It's not just about treating illnesses—it's about preventing them, shifting the healthcare paradigm from reactive to proactive.

AI is doing more than just putting a name on a treatment plan; it's tailoring medical care to the individual characteristics of each patient. By analyzing data from a patient's genetic makeup to their reaction to past treatments, AI can help doctors develop customized treatment plans that are more effective and have fewer side effects. This approach is particularly transformative in fields like oncology, where AI-driven insights can determine which chemotherapy drugs are likely to be most effective for a particular patient's cancer type. Imagine chemotherapy that's potent and personalized, minimizing harm and maximizing healing.

AI acts like the world's most efficient administrative assistant in patient management. It helps schedule appointments, sends reminders to patients, and even helps manage chronic diseases by remotely tracking patient vitals and medication schedules. Wearable devices that monitor everything from heart rate to glucose levels can send real-time data to AI systems, which analyze the data and provide feedback. If a patient's readings are off, the system alerts medical staff and the patient, facilitating timely interventions. This continuous monitoring and real-time data analysis make managing chronic conditions less intrusive and more manageable, keeping patients safe and supported outside the hospital walls.

Ethical Considerations

As much as AI is a boon for healthcare, it brings its own set of ethical questions. Top of the list is patient privacy. With medical data being fed into AI systems, ensuring this information is secured against breaches is paramount.

Then there's the issue of algorithmic bias—AI systems trained on limited or skewed data sets can develop biases that might lead to unequal treatment outcomes. Healthcare professionals must be vigilant, ensuring their AI tools are as unbiased and equitable as possible. Continuous monitoring and updating AI systems with diverse data sets are crucial in mitigating these risks.

Incorporating AI into healthcare isn't just about adopting new technologies; it's a redefinition of care delivery that promises more accuracy, efficiency, efficacy, and personalization. For healthcare professionals, staying abreast of these AI advancements isn't just beneficial—it's essential to providing top-tier care in the modern medical landscape.

As AI continues to evolve, its potential to support both patients and healthcare providers in new and profound ways is boundless. The future of healthcare is here, and AI is its cornerstone, ensuring that care is comprehensive and compassionate.

AI in Education: Teaching and Learning Aids

Imagine walking into a classroom where every student receives personalized guidance, almost as if each had a private tutor. With AI-driven tutoring systems, this is rapidly becoming a reality. These systems are designed to adapt to each student's learning pace and style, providing personalized exercises and feedback to help students master concepts more effectively. If a student struggles with fractions, the AI tutor can offer additional problems and break down the steps more thoroughly, perhaps even offering visual aids or interactive elements to enhance understanding. It's like having a teacher who's always available to give you extra help exactly when you need it.

But AI's role in education isn't limited to just tutoring. It's also transforming how educators handle their day-to-day administrative tasks. Consider teachers' time grading tests, recording attendance, and planning lessons. These are crucial tasks, but they can be repetitive and time-consuming. AI comes to the rescue here by automating many of these administrative duties. For example, AI systems can automatically grade multiple-choice and fill-in-the-blank tests as soon as students submit them. More advanced AI applications are even beginning to help grade more subjective responses and essays, though they're not quite perfect yet. They can also keep track of attendance through simple facial recognition software when students enter the classroom. This automation frees up teachers' time, allowing them to **focus more on teaching and less on paperwork.**

Enhancing classroom engagement is another area where AI is making significant strides. Traditional teaching methods sometimes fail to capture students' interest, leading to disengagement and poor learning outcomes. AI can help create more engaging and interactive learning environments through gamification and virtual reality (VR). Gamification incorporates game design elements in educational settings, making learning fun and motivating students to achieve higher levels.

AI-driven analytics can help tailor these games to each student's learning needs, adjusting the difficulty level and providing new challenges at just the right time. Meanwhile, VR can transport students to different times and places, turning a history lesson into a time travel adventure or a biology lesson into a journey inside the human body. These technologies make learning more engaging and enhance students' understanding by providing them with immersive, first-hand experiences of the material.

Preparing students for an AI-driven world is perhaps one of the most crucial tasks educators face today. As AI technology becomes more pervasive across different sectors, the workforce of the future will need to adapt to new challenges and work alongside AI. Educators need to start incorporating AI education into their curricula, teaching students how to use AI tools and understand and interact with AI ethically and effectively.

This can be as simple as introducing students to basic AI concepts and applications or as involved as setting up specialized courses on AI and machine learning. Moreover, educators should encourage students to think critically about AI's implications, including privacy, bias, and ethics. By integrating AI education into school curricula, educators can prepare students not just to navigate a world where AI is common but also to lead in shaping its development and ensuring it's used responsibly.

Incorporating AI into education offers a multitude of benefits, from personalized learning and administrative efficiency to enhanced engagement and preparedness for the future. As these technologies continue to evolve, their potential to transform the educational landscape becomes increasingly profound. For educators and students alike, understanding and utilizing AI tools isn't just about keeping up with technological advancements—it's about redefining what education can achieve. As we continue to explore the possibilities, the role of AI in education is set to grow, promising more personalized, engaging, and compelling learning experiences for students worldwide.

AI in Agriculture: Tech Meets Tradition

Imagine a world where every plant in a vast field gets exactly the amount of water it needs, no more, no less. Or picture a fleet of robots gently picking apples, navigating between rows with the grace of a seasoned farmer. This might sound like scenes from a futuristic movie, but it's the reality of modern agriculture thanks to AI. The merging of technology with traditional farming techniques, often referred to as precision agriculture, is revolutionizing how we grow food, making farming more efficient, sustainable, and kind to our planet.

Precision Agriculture

Precision agriculture is all about making farming smarter. Traditional farming methods often involve a one-size-fits-all approach—like watering an entire field at the same rate without considering each plant. AI changes the game by enabling what's known as precision agriculture. This technique uses data from various sources, such as satellites, drones, or soil sensors, to monitor the condition of crops and soil at a very granular level. AI analyzes this data and provides insights into which parts of a field need more water or fertilizer. Farmers can then target specific field areas with the amount of water, fertilizers, or pesticides needed, reducing waste and increasing yields. It's like giving each plant its personalized care, ensuring they grow healthy and strong, which is good for the farmer's bottom line and the environment.

The impact? Sustainability. Water usage is cut dramatically, and that is crucial in water scarcity areas. By applying the right amount of water where and when needed, farmers can conserve water while maintaining high crop yields. Reducing the runoff from overwatering means fewer pollutants in rivers and lakes. It's a win-win: better for the earth and better for the farmers.

Robotics in Farming

AI-powered robots are stepping up as agricultural aides, doing everything from planting and weeding to harvesting. Robots can plant seeds precisely, reducing seed waste and optimizing plant spacing. Weeding looks completely different, imagine tiny robots scuttling between crops, using AI to differentiate between weed and plant. Save hours of manual labor and reduce the need for chemical herbicides, another bonus for eco-friendly farming.

Harvesting is where robots truly shine. They can be equipped with AI to assess the ripeness of fruits and vegetables, picking them at the perfect moment. This task requires a delicate touch and a good bit of judgment, which is traditionally the role of human farmers, but AI robots are quickly learning the ropes. Their efficiency can drastically cut down on labor costs and address the challenges posed by labor shortages in agriculture, all while ensuring that the produce is of the highest quality.

AI helps before the seeds hit the soil. Predictive analytics in agriculture uses AI to process data from various sources to predict crop outcomes. This can include predicting the best planting dates and anticipating potential disease outbreaks before any visible signs appear. By analyzing weather data, soil conditions, crop history, and satellite images, AI can help farmers make informed decisions that increase crop success rates.

For example, if AI predicts a high likelihood of a particular pest outbreak based on current climate conditions and historical data, farmers can proactively treat crops at just the right time to prevent widespread damage. This ensures the quality of the produce, and significantly impact yield.

Sustainability: AI in agriculture is not just about boosting productivity and profits; it's about ensuring sustainable farming practices for generations to come. By optimizing resources and reducing reliance on chemical pesticides and fertilizers, AI helps create farming practices that are more in harmony with the environment. AI-driven farming can lead to more resilient food systems, improving yield forecasts' accuracy and enabling better management of food supply chains. This is crucial for feeding a growing global population in a way that doesn't deplete our planet's resources.

In essence, AI is planting the seeds for a future where farming is not only more productive and profitable but also kinder to the planet. This exemplifies how tradition and technology can create something truly revolutionary. As we continue to explore and expand the use of AI in agriculture, the promise of feeding the world in a sustainable, efficient, and environmentally friendly way becomes increasingly within reach. From precision agriculture to robotic farmhands and predictive analytics, AI is truly transforming agriculture.

AI in Customer Service: Enhancing User Experience

Imagine you're in a bustling coffee shop, trying to order your favorite brew during the morning rush. The line is long, the staff is swamped, and you wish for a magic button to speed things up. Well, in the world of customer service, AI-powered chatbots and virtual assistants are that magic button. They're like the super-efficient barista who knows your regular order, manages the queue, and ensures everyone leaves with a smile, all at lightning speed!

Let's start with chatbots. I suspect chatbots are what most skeptics and beginners complain about. These AI-driven helpers are revolutionizing customer service by quickly and accurately responding to customer inquiries; however, if you are used to talking to someone, a chatbot seems inferior to a conversation. They are here to stay. I like to message companies during off-hours using the chat feature, which these days always begins with a chatbot: "Is this your issue this or that/," "If this, then that." Sound familiar? Just be patient, follow along and before you know it, if need be, a human being will step in. You have to surrender to the fact that this is the way it is. You might as well create a way to be effective versus letting that voice take over; on going learning and adapting to your ever-changing environment is key.

Whether it's a question about a product, a service issue, or just needing guidance on a website, chatbots are there to help at any time of the day or night. What makes them so efficient? They're powered by natural language processing (NLP) systems that understand human language, not just commands but also the nuances of human conversation. This means they can engage in a way that feels natural and helpful rather than robotic and frustrating.

Think of a chatbot as a friendly guide in the complex customer service maze. They can handle a multitude of queries simultaneously, reducing wait times and freeing up human agents to tackle more complex issues. This speeds up service and improves the overall customer experience, making interactions smoother and more satisfying. Plus, they learn from each interaction, constantly improving their responses and understanding of customer needs. It's like having a customer service agent who gets better every day without ever needing a break!

Moving on to personalization, AI takes customer service to a whole new level. By analyzing data from past interactions, purchases, and even browsing patterns, AI can tailor conversations and recommendations to each individual customer. This isn't about addressing someone by their name; it's about understanding their preferences and history with your company and even anticipating their needs before they articulate them.

If a customer frequently buys eco-friendly products, AI can highlight new green products or suggest eco-friendly alternatives. This personalized interaction could make customers feel valued and understood, enhancing their loyalty to your brand. It's like having a personal shopper for each customer who remembers every interaction and uses that knowledge to improve each experience.

Automating Routine Tasks

While necessary, routine tasks can be time-consuming and monotonous. AI excels at automating these tasks, such as sorting through tickets, prioritizing responses based on urgency, and even managing inventory inquiries. Automating these processes allows human agents to focus on providing more personalized, high-value interactions where empathy and human judgment are crucial.

AI can manage these tasks around the clock, without pause, ensuring that customer service is a 24/7 operation. This means that no matter when a customer reaches out, be it midnight or early morning, their queries are handled efficiently. This constant availability improves customer satisfaction and boosts your company's reputation as responsive and reliable.

Lastly, AI's role in training and quality assurance in customer service is unprecedented. Through sentiment analysis and feedback evaluation, AI tools can monitor customer interaction quality and provide agents with real-time coaching. For instance, if an interaction is veering off-course, AI can suggest real-time tips to the agent on how to steer it back to a positive outcome.

AI also plays a crucial role in training new customer service agents. By analyzing data from thousands of past interactions, AI can identify the most effective communication strategies and common customer issues, creating a training program that's both comprehensive and deeply informed by real-world data. This ensures that new agents are not only well-prepared but are also more consistent in delivering high-quality service.

Incorporating AI into customer service doesn't just transform operations; it makes them smarter, faster, and more personalized. From chatbots handling routine queries to AI personalizing customer interactions and automating mundane tasks, AI empowers businesses to deliver exceptional service. Moreover, its training and quality assurance role ensures that customer service teams are always at their best, continuously improving and adapting to meet customer needs.

AI is not about replacing the human touch; it's about enhancing it. It's about giving you the tools to meet your customers' needs more effectively, making every interaction a stepping stone to greater customer satisfaction and loyalty. So, embrace AI and watch as it transforms your customer service into a powerhouse of efficiency and personalization. Ready to see how AI is revolutionizing other industries?

Chapter Seven

The Future of AI and You

E ver feel like you stepped into a sci-fi novel every time you hear about AI doing something mind-blowingly advanced? We're about to dive into one of AI's most thrilling co-stars: quantum computing. This isn't just any tech fling; it's the kind of partnership that could catapult AI into new realms of possibilities, solving problems faster than you can snap your fingers!

Understanding Quantum Computing and AI

Let's start with a quick trip down Quantum Lane. Imagine if, instead of deciding between yes or no, on or off, like the bits in classical computers, you could choose both simultaneously. That's the quantum world, where a quantum bit, or qubit, can exist in multiple states at once thanks to superposition. Now, add another mind-boggling feature: entanglement, where qubits, no matter how far apart, can be intertwined so that the state of one (whether it's on or off) can depend on the state of another. This kind of weirdness not only baffles the mind but also powers quantum computers to perform complex calculations at speeds unattainable by their classical counterparts.

AI processes massive amounts of data to learn and make decisions. It's like having a super-fast student who can read a library of books in seconds. But even this super-student has limits, especially when faced with complex problems that would take years to solve with conventional computers. Enter quantum computing. Quantum computers could dramatically speed up AI's data processing by performing multiple calculations simultaneously. AI could learn and evolve at rates we've hardly dared to imagine, tackling problems like simulating molecular structures for drug discovery or optimizing vast logistics networks with unprecedented efficiency.

As you read this, researchers are bustling in labs worldwide, pushing the boundaries of what quantum computers can do. Organizations from Google to IBM and various startups are in a thrilling race to harness quantum computing for AI. They are exploring everything from quantum algorithms that can accelerate machine learning to quantum circuits that could be the building blocks of new forms of AI. It's a bubbling pot of innovation, where each breakthrough brings us closer to a future where AI might help us cure diseases, stabilize climate change, or even unravel mysteries of the universe.

Let your imagination run wild for a moment. Picture a world where AI, powered by quantum computing, predicts weather patterns with pinpoint accuracy, helping us better prepare for natural disasters. Or envision AI designing new materials with atomic precision, leading to lighter, stronger, and more sustainable products. In finance, quantum

AI could simulate market conditions so detailed that economic forecasts become nearly as reliable as tomorrow's weather predictions. These scenarios might sound like pages from a futuristic novel, but with quantum computing, they could become tomorrow's headlines.

Interactive Element: Quantum Leap Quiz

Think you've got a handle on quantum computing? Test your knowledge with this quick quiz:

What allows quantum bits to be more powerful than classical bits?

1. Superposition

2. Entanglement

3. Both of the above

4. None of the above

Which field could benefit most immediately from quantum computing?

1. Drug discovery

2. Traffic light timing

3. Online shopping

4. All of the above

Whether you got them right or were a bit off the mark, remember every bit of curiosity brings you closer to understanding the incredible potential of AI and quantum computing. The answers are 3 and 1.

As we continue to explore the intertwining paths of AI and quantum computing, remember, you're not just passively observing this exciting journey—you're part of a generation that might see some of the most outstanding scientific and technological achievements in human history. Stay curious, stay engaged, and who knows? You might be part of the next big AI and quantum computing breakthrough.

AI and the Internet of Things: A Connected World

Imagine your morning starts not with you checking all the household gadgets but with those gadgets taking care of themselves. Your coffee starts brewing when your alarm goes off, the thermostat adjusts to a cozy temperature just as your feet hit the floor, and your car warms up in the driveway, ready for the commute. This isn't a scene from a futuristic movie; it's the power of AI integrated with the Internet of Things (IoT), transforming our living spaces, cities, and industries into more imaginative, more responsive environments.

The concept might sound a bit tech-heavy, so let's break it down a bit. IoT refers to the network of physical objects—"things"—embedded with sensors, software, and other technologies to connect and exchange data with other devices and systems over the internet. AI enhances these capabilities by enabling these devices to analyze the data they collect and make intelligent decisions locally. For example, consider a smart thermostat that learns your schedule and temperature preferences. Over time, it gathers data, understands your habits, and adjusts the temperature, ensuring maximum comfort while optimizing energy use.

Integrating AI with IoT is not just about making life easier. It's reshaping entire industries and communities. Take smart cities, for example. Urban areas worldwide are becoming smarter by embedding AI into their IoT infrastructure. Traffic lights adjust to traffic conditions, minimizing congestion and reducing emissions. Public safety improves with smart surveillance systems that can identify incidents and deploy emergency services faster than ever before. Then there's healthcare, where AI-powered health monitoring devices worn on the wrist can track heart rates, predict potential health issues, and even alert doctors, providing a new level of proactive healthcare management.

In the industrial sector, AI and IoT are revolutionizing traditional practices. Automated factory systems can predict when machines need maintenance long before a breakdown occurs, minimizing downtime and saving money. These systems can also optimize production schedules and supply chains, making them more efficient and less prone to human error. It's like having a super-efficient assistant who keeps everything running smoothly and anticipates problems before they arise.

The perks of marrying AI with IoT are plentiful. Efficiency is a major one—systems can automate tasks and process information much faster than humans, reducing waste and increasing productivity. Personalization is another; devices learn from individual interactions and adjust to user preferences, providing a tailored experience, whether in adjusting home lighting or suggesting a new coffee flavor based on previous choices. Let's not forget about enhanced decision-making; with more accurate and timely information at their fingertips, humans can make informed decisions quickly, whether navigating through traffic or managing a vast network of industrial machines.

Of course, integrating AI with IoT isn't without its challenges, security being one and high on the list. With billions of devices connected and communicating, the risk of data breaches increases. Ensuring these devices are secure and the data they collect is protected is paramount. Privacy is another concern. As devices collect and analyze more personal data, ensuring this information is used ethically and responsibly is crucial. Lastly, there's the challenge of infrastructure. For AI and IoT to work together seamlessly, robust network systems must be in place to handle vast amounts of data being processed and shared.

As we navigate these challenges and harness the benefits, the fusion of AI and IoT stands to redefine our interactions with technology. From homes that manage themselves to cities that think like a brain, the integration of AI and IoT sets the stage for a more innovative, more connected world. So, the next time you enjoy a perfectly brewed cup of coffee just as you like it right when you wake up, take a moment to appreciate the sophisticated dance of AI and IoT happening right under your nose, quietly and efficiently making your day better.

The Role of AI in Sustainable Practices

Imagine a world where our forests are monitored with such precision that we can almost hear the whispers of the trees, telling us precisely what they need to thrive and how they're coping with environmental stresses. This is a real possibility with AI stepping into the role of guardian of our natural world. AI's ability to digest large amounts of data from satellites, drones, and ground sensors makes it a powerful ally in environmental conservation. For instance, AI systems can monitor deforestation activities, providing alerts when unusual patterns are detected. This allows for quicker response, potentially stopping illegal logging activities before they cause too much damage. AI aids in tracking wildlife, using algorithms to analyze images from camera traps to monitor animal populations and behaviors without human interference. This provides more accurate data and ensures a safer environment for animals and conservationists.

When predicting natural disasters, AI's predictive prowess is like having a crystal ball that offers a glimpse into possible future scenarios based on current environmental data. Whether forecasting the path of hurricanes or predicting areas at risk of wildfires, AI enhances our preparedness and response strategies. This proactive approach saves countless lives and mitigates economic impacts, allowing for better resource allocation before, during, and after disasters. It's as if AI has given us the ability to speak the language of the planet, enabling us to listen and respond more effectively to its needs.

Switching gears to energy efficiency, AI's role is akin to that of an energy auditor for various sectors, constantly searching for ways to cut waste and enhance efficiency. From smart grids that adjust the flow of electricity based on demand to intelligent building systems that learn optimal energy use patterns, AI is reshaping how we consume energy. In factories, AI systems optimize machine use, reducing idle times and predicting maintenance needs to prevent energy-sapping breakdowns. On a larger scale, AI manages renewable energy sources, analyzing weather data to predict solar and wind power availability, thus balancing the grid by deciding when to store energy or feed it into the system, maximizing the use of renewable resources, and reducing reliance on fossil fuels, steering us closer to a sustainable energy future.

AI revolutionizes resource management, turning what used to be a game of educated guesses into a data-driven strategy. Water management is a prime example. AI models predict water demand across cities, adjusting supply to avoid shortages and wastage. These systems can also detect leaks and predict pipe failures before they happen, preserving precious water resources and saving money on repairs. In waste management, AI sorts recyclables from waste with precision, improving recycling rates and reducing landfill use. Moreover, AI platforms analyze waste generation patterns, helping cities optimize collection routes and schedules and reduce fuel consumption and emissions from waste collection vehicles.

AI's potential to propel sustainable development goals (SDGs) cannot be overstressed. By aligning AI strategies with SDGs, we can leverage this technology to address global challenges such as hunger, poverty, and climate change. AI-driven agricultural technologies increase crop yields and reduce resources, supporting sustainable agriculture practices. In urban development, AI tools optimize everything from traffic flows to public services, making cities more livable and efficient. AI improves disease surveillance and diagnostics in healthcare, especially in under-resourced areas, bridging the gap in global health services. AI supports specific SDGs through these applications and fosters an integrated approach to sustainability, emphasizing interconnectivity and synergy across various sectors.

In each of these roles, AI emerges not just as a tool of convenience but as a catalyst for profound change, driving us towards a future where sustainability is not just an ideal but a practical, integral part of everyday life. As we continue to explore and innovate, the fusion of AI with sustainability efforts promises to protect and nurture our planet and redefine our legacy as stewards of a world that thrives on synergy, balance, and forward-thinking stewardship.

Future AI Technologies in Everyday Life

Imagine a world where your car drives you to work while you catch up on your favorite series or prepare for an important meeting. It's the direction we're heading with advancements in autonomous vehicles. These marvels of modern technology are navigating complex urban environments more safely and efficiently than ever. Integrating advanced sensors, machine learning algorithms, and vast amounts of data has enabled these vehicles to understand and react to their surroundings, drastically reducing human errors that lead to accidents. The impact on daily commutes and urban planning is profound. Cities could see a significant decrease in traffic congestion as autonomous vehicles communicate with each other to optimize traffic flow. Parking lots could become obsolete as self-driving cars drop passengers off and park in remote locations. The ripple effects extend to reduced pollution and increased productivity as commuting time transforms into a productive part of the day.

Transitioning from autonomous cars to personal AI assistants, these handy helpers are set to become even more intuitive and proactive in managing our daily lives. Imagine your AI assistant not just responding to commands but anticipating your needs. It might suggest leaving early for your appointment if there's heavy traffic or rescheduling your meetings if a personal emergency arises. These assistants could evolve to manage complex tasks like budgeting or event planning, learning from each interaction to better serve your needs. The key to this evolution is the integration of AI with big data and predictive analytics, allowing these systems to understand patterns in your behavior and make increasingly accurate predictions about your preferences and needs. This personalized assistance could extend beyond mere convenience, offering support in managing mental health, reminding you to take breaks, or suggesting activities based on the patterns it notices in your stress levels or mood fluctuations.

AI in personal health is a field on the brink of revolutionary change. Future developments in AI-driven health monitoring and management promise to extend far beyond the current capabilities of fitness trackers and health apps. Imagine a system that tracks your vitals and predicts potential health issues before they arise, using sophisticated algorithms to analyze trends in your biometric data. This system could alert you and your doctor to early signs of conditions like heart disease or diabetes, enabling preventative treatment to save millions of lives and billions of dollars in healthcare costs annually. Moreover, powered by AI, the future of personalized medicine could tailor treatments to your genetic profile, significantly increasing their effectiveness. AI could design customized fitness and nutrition programs that adapt to your body's responses, optimizing your health in a way that general advice could never achieve.

Given the evolution of smart homes, the future looks incredibly convenient, comfortable, and energy-efficient. AI is set to take home automation to new heights with systems that adjust everything from lighting and temperature to entertainment and security based on your habits and preferences. Your home could recognize your mood through voice and posture analysis and adjust lighting and music to soothe or energize you or play meditative music and sounds. AI could also manage your home's energy consumption more efficiently than ever, using data to balance the electricity load and integrate seamlessly with renewable energy sources. Your home could become an automated environment that responds to your commands and anticipates your needs, ensuring optimal comfort while minimizing energy.

As we look toward these developments, it's clear that AI is set to deeply integrate into every aspect of our lives, making our days more productive, our decisions more informed, and our environments more comfortable. The potential is limitless, and while there are challenges to navigate, particularly around privacy and data security, the benefits could reshape our world in ways we are just beginning to imagine.

Preparing for a Career in an AI-Driven Future

Navigating a career in a landscape where AI plays a starring role might feel like trying to dance on a constantly shifting stage. But here's the kicker: it's not just about keeping your balance but learning new moves. As AI reshapes industries, the demand for specific skills is shooting up faster than a rocket. We're talking about capabilities like AI ethics, system integration, and AI maintenance. Let's briefly look at these skills.

Starting with AI ethics, it's not just about programming or data crunching; it's about ensuring AI behaves well in the sandbox with the rest of us. Ethical concerns are skyrocketing with AI integrated into everything from healthcare to finance. How do we ensure AI decisions are fair? What happens if an AI system goes rogue? Professionals skilled in AI ethics are the new guardians of technology, ensuring AI solutions are developed and deployed responsibly, respecting privacy, fairness, and transparency. Imagine being the person who ensures AI doesn't just work efficiently but also fairly and kindly. This role isn't just important; it's essential as we lean more on AI in critical areas of our lives.

Then there's system integration – the art of blending AI with existing tech systems. It's like being a tech chef, mixing ingredients (AI systems) not initially designed to work together into a seamless recipe that boosts business efficiency and innovation. As more companies adopt AI, the need for pros who can integrate new AI tools with old systems, ensuring they communicate smoothly, is skyrocketing. Whether automating data entry or streamlining manufacturing processes, integration specialists ensure that AI solutions fit perfectly within the broader tech ecosystem of a business, enhancing functionality without disrupting existing operations.

AI maintenance, Just like cars, AI systems need tune-ups to run smoothly. This involves regular updates, managing data flows, and ensuring the AI adapts to new data or goals. AI maintenance professionals keep the AI engines running smoothly, diagnosing and fixing issues before they become problems. This role is crucial because even the most innovative AI can start to underperform if it's not maintained correctly. Think of yourself as an AI mechanic, keeping everything running smoothly and tweaking the system for optimal performance.

Mastering these skills is one thing, but staying relevant in a rapidly evolving job market is another. This is where lifelong learning and adaptability come into play. The AI field isn't just changing; it's growing, and yesterday's knowledge might not solve tomorrow's challenges. Embracing lifelong learning is like keeping your toolbox stocked with the latest gadgets. Whether through online courses, workshops, or new degree programs, continuously updating your skills ensures you stay valuable and versatile in a job market where change is the only constant.

Why stop at one discipline? The future belongs to those who can look across the boundaries of technology, arts, biology, and more. Cross-disciplinary learning is about connecting the dots between AI and other fields. Imagine using AI to analyze genetic data to tailor medical treatments or AI-driven analytics to enhance creative designs in art. By blending AI knowledge with expertise in other areas, you create a unique skill set that can push innovation in ways that staying within traditional boundaries never could.

As you gear up to ride the AI wave, don't forget the power of networking and community engagement. Diving into professional networks and communities focused on AI can open doors to opportunities you might not find elsewhere. That devil, FaceBook, has many AI groups and experience levels. From online forums and LinkedIn groups to local meet-ups and conferences, connecting with peers, mentors, and industry leaders can provide insights, advice, and partnerships that propel your career forward. It's not just about what you know; it's also about who you know and who knows you. Engaging actively with the AI community can turn the daunting task of keeping up with AI advancements into an exciting collaborative journey.

As you ponder the future of AI and your place in it, remember that preparing for a career in this dynamic field is about more than just technical skills. It's about ethical understanding, integration savvy, maintenance know-how, lifelong learning, interdisciplinary thinking, and community engagement. By nurturing these areas, you equip yourself to participate in the future and help shape it. Whether you're steering AI projects in ethical directions, integrating cutting-edge AI systems, keeping complex AI operations running smoothly, or breaking new ground by linking AI with other disciplines, your journey in the AI-driven landscape is just beginning. So, keep learning, keep connecting, and keep pushing the boundaries. The future isn't just happening; you're helping to create it.

How to Stay Up to Date with AI Advancements

Keeping up with AI isn't just about staying relevant; it's like being a surfer where the waves are these constant innovations and breakthroughs—you must keep paddling to ride them! Whether you're a complete newbie to the AI scene or someone who's dabbled a bit, the digital world offers a treasure trove of resources that can keep you clued in and ready to dive deeper. Let's explore how you can stay plugged into the ever-evolving world of AI without feeling overwhelmed.

AI is a fast-paced field, and keeping up can sometimes feel like trying to drink from a fire hose. Start by identifying a few essential blogs and websites that resonate with your interests. Websites like 'Towards Data Science' on Medium offer many articles ranging from beginner guides to in-depth discussions on the latest AI research. They break down complex AI concepts, making them perfect for easing into the vast ocean of AI knowledge. Then, there are platforms like TechCrunch and Wired, where you can get the latest news on tech advancements and AI applications across different industries. For those who prefer a more academic approach, journals like 'Journal of Artificial Intelligence Research' or 'AI Magazine' can be goldmines of information, offering peer-reviewed papers and state-of-the-art research findings.

Imagine if you could read about AI and interact with the people shaping its future. Attending AI conferences and workshops can be an exhilarating experience. These events bring together thought leaders, innovators, and researchers from around the globe. You get to witness the unveiling of new technologies firsthand, participate in workshops, and even pitch your questions during panel discussions. Not to mention, the networking opportunities are invaluable. You could be sipping coffee next to the next big AI startup founder or a pioneer in machine learning. Start with popular conferences like NeurIPS, ICML (International Conference on Machine Learning), or local tech meetups in your area. Many conferences offer virtual attendance options now so that you can join from anywhere worldwide!

Utilizing Online Learning Resources

The internet is your best friend for those who love a structured learning approach. Online platforms like Coursera, Udacity, and edX offer courses designed by experts from top universities and tech companies. Whether you want to start with 'AI for Everyone' or tackle something more advanced like 'Deep Learning Specialization,' these platforms have you covered. Most courses include interactive elements like forums, peer-reviewed assignments, and even real-world projects, providing a comprehensive learning experience. And the best part? You can learn at your own pace, fitting AI mastery into your schedule however it works best for you.

Dive into the vibrant world of AI communities online. Platforms like GitHub or Stack Overflow are bustling with enthusiasts and professionals who share your interests. Join discussions, contribute to open-source projects, or follow along with trending topics to see what's sparking interest in the AI world. These communities are about learning, contributing, sharing, and growing together. Whether troubleshooting a coding issue or seeking career advice, you'll find a community ready to support and inspire you.

Staying updated with AI advancements means more than keeping tabs on the latest technologies. It's about actively participating in the learning and development processes that shape AI's role in our world. By engaging with educational resources, connecting with communities, and keeping a finger on the pulse of AI research and news, you're not just a bystander in AI—you're a part of its ongoing evolution. So, keep exploring, keep learning, and who knows? Maybe you'll be the one leading the next big AI breakthrough.

As we wrap up this chapter on staying current with AI advancements, remember that the journey into AI is as exciting as it is transformative. Through the avenues discussed, from engaging with online communities to participating in global conferences, you're not just keeping up—you're actively shaping your understanding and influence in AI. As we move forward, carry this proactive spirit into the next chapter, where we'll explore the fascinating intersections of AI with other cutting-edge technologies. Stay curious, stay engaged, and let's continue unraveling AI's marvels together.

Chapter Eight

Building Your AI Journey

T hink of AI not as a vast, uncharted universe but more like your neighborhood coffee shop where every visit makes you a tad more familiar with the menu. Here, we'll start by figuring out what 'flavor' of AI suits you best, chart a path to your learning, and even make sure you can measure how much you're enjoying the brew along the way!

Setting Up Your AI Learning Path

Knowing your starting point is crucial before you sprint down the AI track. Are you a complete novice who gets jittery at mentioning algorithms? Or have you dabbled a bit, perhaps tried out a few basic tools or read some introductory articles? Understanding your current knowledge level helps sculpt a learning path that's not too steep or gentle. Think of it like choosing the right difficulty level in a video game; the better the fit, the more engaging the experience.

Here's a fun way to gauge your level: consider how you interact with your smartphone or computer. Are you the go-to person in your family for tech support, or does the idea of updating software fill you with dread? Your comfort with technology can be a good indicator of your foundational skills for diving into AI.

Let's talk goals. And no, I don't mean those lofty 'I want to be the next Elon Musk' kinds of goals (though dreaming big is a good habit), but relatively small, achievable targets. Setting realistic goals is like placing markers on a hiking trail; they keep you motivated and moving in the right direction. Maybe you start with understanding the basics of AI—what it is, what it's not, and some common uses. Next, you might aim to complete a basic online course or build a simple AI model. Long-term, perhaps you aspire to integrate AI into your workplace or start a project that impacts your community. Remember, the beauty of learning AI is that it's as much about the journey as it is about the destination.

Crafting a personalized learning plan is like sketching a treasure map where X marks your unique version of success. Start by listing areas of AI that intrigue you—be it ethical implications, creative applications like AI in music and art, or technical aspects like machine learning and neural networks. Next, align these interests with your goals to create a learning roadmap. For instance, if you're ethical, you might prioritize courses and content focusing on AI's societal impacts. Or, if you're artistically inclined, exploring AI tools that assist in digital art could be your starting point. The key is to tailor this plan to your pace and interests, ensuring it remains flexible to accommodate new interests or shifts in focus as you progress.

Keeping track of your progress is crucial and can be incredibly rewarding. Simple tools like learning diaries or progress bars in online courses can help. Or, why not go techy with a custom dashboard using basic coding? Platforms like GitHub or even spreadsheet software can help you visualize milestones. Regularly update your achievements, no matter how small—it could be completing a chapter in a book or a section in an online course. Watching your progress visually accumulate over time isn't just motivating; it also solidifies your learning and gives you tangible proof of how far you've come.

Why not start an AI learning journal to make this journey truly yours? Here's your first prompt: Write about what AI means to you now and what you hope it will mean for you by the end of your learning path. This sets a personal benchmark and will be a fascinating snippet to look back on as you advance. By understanding your starting point, setting clear goals, customizing your learning path, and tracking your progress, you're not just preparing for a successful journey into AI—you're setting the stage for a transformation in how you interact with technology and the world around you. So, grab your metaphorical backpack; let's start your AI adventure with all the right tools!

Resources and Communities for AI Enthusiasts

Navigating the vast seas of AI resources might initially seem like trying to find a needle in a digital haystack. Fear not! Picture this: a treasure map leading you to golden nuggets of AI knowledge scattered across the internet and beyond. First up, let's talk about online platforms. MOOCs (Massive Open Online Courses) such as Coursera, edX, and Udacity offer many courses designed to take you from AI novice to AI savvy in no time. These platforms collaborate with universities and tech companies to provide courses in everything from basic AI principles to advanced machine learning techniques. Whether you want to understand AI ethics or get hands-on with deep learning, these courses are structured to provide comprehensive learning at your own pace. They often include interactive forums to ask questions and exchange ideas with fellow learners worldwide.

If you're more of a do it-yourself learner, specialized AI training websites like Fast.ai and DeepLearning.ai throw you into the deep end of AI through practical, project-based learning. Here, it's less about passing exams and more about actually building something with what you learn. For those who prefer a more structured academic environment, many top universities now offer their AI courses online for free or for a fee. Stanford University's Machine Learning by Andrew Ng (available on Coursera) is an exemplary course that has helped countless enthusiasts grasp the complex algorithms of AI.

Let's shift gears to books and publications because the good old-fashioned written word still holds powerful sway in the age of digital flashes and clicks. For starters, "Artificial Intelligence: A Guide for Thinking Humans" by Melanie Mitchell provides an insightful exploration of AI's capabilities and challenges, making it accessible without needing a PhD. If you're looking for something more technical, "Deep Learning" by Ian Goodfellow, Yoshua Bengio, and Aaron Courville dives deep into the methods and mathematics of building machine learning systems.

AI doesn't have to be a solitary journey. Joining AI communities can alter your learning path from a monologue to a vibrant dialogue. Platforms like Meetup.com offer a variety of AI and machine learning groups, where you can find everything from beginner-friendly gatherings to advanced workshops. Online forums like Stack Overflow and GitHub provide platforms to troubleshoot code, collaborate on projects, share insights, and keep up with the latest trends. Social media groups are bustling hubs where AI enthusiasts gather to share articles, discuss new developments, and network.

Leveraging community knowledge can significantly amplify your learning experience. Imagine working on a project and getting stuck—instead of banging your head against the virtual wall, you can reach out to the community. More often than not, someone has faced the same issue and can provide a solution or offer a new perspective you hadn't considered. These interactions frequently lead to opportunities for collaborative projects that can be more ambitious than solo endeavors. Such collaborations enhance your practical skills and deepen your understanding as you explain concepts, debate approaches, and share failures and successes.

In these communities, mentorship plays a pivotal role, too. Experienced professionals often provide guidance to help steer your learning journey and offer career advice. Sometimes, if you're lucky, they might open doors to opportunities that can accelerate your career in AI. Engaging actively within these communities, contributing to discussions, and sharing your learning cements your knowledge and establishes your presence in AI. So, as you step forward, remember that every post you read, course, and discussion you engage in weaves another thread into the rich tapestry of your AI education.

Tackling AI can sometimes feel like you're trying to solve a Rubik's cube—blindfolded. It's easy to get tangled in the complex concepts, mathematical formulas, and the sheer amount of resources available. But every AI guru started somewhere. Let's look at some common roadblocks you might encounter and arm you with strategies to jump over them with grace.

First up, the complexity of concepts in AI can be pretty daunting. It's like trying to understand an inside joke in a language you barely speak. But here's the kicker: you don't need to learn everything in one go. Break down big, scary AI topics into bite-sized pieces. Tackle one small topic at a time, and give yourself the chance to digest it thoroughly before moving on. Think of it as eating an elephant one bite at a time! Start with basic terminology and gradually work up to more complex theories. Online platforms often segment learning into manageable modules, which can be incredibly helpful. Also, don't shy away from using analogies and real-life examples to wrap your head around abstract concepts. If 'neural networks' sound baffling, think of them as a busy post office, sorting and directing information to where it needs to go.

AI and machine learning do involve a fair bit of math. It can be a hurdle if you're not confident in your mathematical skills. However, not all AI pathways require you to be a math wizard. Initially, focus on understanding the concepts rather than the intricate mathematical details. Use tools and software that handle the heavy math for you. As you grow more comfortable, you can delve deeper into the algorithms and calculus if you choose. Meanwhile, platforms like Khan Academy can be great for brushing up on specific math skills at your own pace.

Resource overload is another speed bump on the road to AI mastery. The internet is a treasure trove of courses, books, tutorials, and more—where do you even start? It's crucial to curate your resources. Not all that glitters in your Google search results is gold. Start with well-reviewed and recommended resources. Lean on community forums and trusted AI blogs to see what seasoned AI enthusiasts suggest. And remember, it's okay to be picky with what you choose to spend your time on. Trying something else is fine if a resource isn't clicking with you. Sometimes, the right teaching style can make all the difference.

Maintaining motivation might be your biggest challenge. Learning AI isn't always going to be a walk in the park. There will be frustrating moments, but setting small, achievable milestones can help immensely. Think of these like mini-celebrations on your path to AI fluency. Have you completed a challenging module? Give yourself a pat on the back, or treat yourself to a nice coffee. Keep a visual track of your progress. I can't say this enough: maybe a chart on your wall or a progress thread in an online community. Seeing how far you've come can be a huge boost, and sharing your progress with others can spark encouragement and advice for the next steps.

Finally, adapting your learning methods can significantly smoothen your AI learning curve. We all learn differently—some like to dive straight in, while others prefer to start with conceptual frameworks or watch interactive simulations. If you're hands-on, try small projects like building a simple chatbot or using AI tools in photo editing software if you're more theoretically inclined, deep-dive into case studies or academic papers on AI applications. The key is to find what works for you. Experiment with different methods and tools until you find your 'learning groove.'

Navigating the complexities of AI learning isn't just about hard work; it's about intelligent strategies, patience, and a bit of creativity in how you approach problems. With these tactics, the once-daunting world of AI becomes a playground of opportunities. So, gear up, use these strategies, and turn those AI lemons into zesty lemonade!

DIY Next Steps in Hands-on Learning

So, you've got a handle on the basics of AI, and now you're itching to roll up your sleeves and actually build something. Perfect! Let's turn those theoretical gears into practical outcomes. Starting with DIY AI projects not only cements your learning but can also be incredibly satisfying—there's nothing quite like seeing your digital creation come to life.

Let's spark some ideas. How about building a simple AI that predicts your weekly grocery expenses based on your past shopping habits? Or maybe a more ambitious project like a chatbot that helps users learn a new language? The beauty of these projects is that they can be as straightforward or as complex as you're comfortable with. Creating a basic recommendation system might sound fancy for beginners, but it's quite doable. This system could recommend movies or books based on what you've liked in the past, using data you provide about your preferences.

How do you build one of these projects? Let's walk through setting up a basic recommendation system. First, gather your data. This could be a list of movies you've watched with ratings you've given them. Next, choose a tool. With its rich libraries and community support, Python is a fantastic choice for beginners. Using Python, you can leverage libraries like Pandas for data handling and Scikit-learn to build recommendation logic. Start by loading your data, then use a simple algorithm like k-nearest neighbors to find similar movies. Finally, test it out! Input a few movies you like and see what the system recommends.

But where do you get these tools? This is where open-source platforms shine. Tools like TensorFlow and Scikit-learn are not just powerful. They're also free and backed by thriving communities. TensorFlow, for instance, excels in handling large datasets and neural network-based projects. It might be a bit of a curve to understand it entirely, but the documentation and community forums are treasure troves of knowledge and examples. Scikit-learn, on the other hand, is excellent for beginners looking to implement more straightforward machine learning algorithms, which is perfect for our recommendation system.

Once you've built your project, why keep it to yourself? Please share it with the AI community. Platforms like GitHub let you showcase your work and open it up to feedback from fellow enthusiasts and experts. This can be invaluable. Feedback might help you fine-tune your project or inspire new features and improvements. Plus, contributing projects to the community can help others learn and might even catch the eye of potential employers or collaborators. Imagine teaming up with someone halfway worldwide to polish your project or integrate new exciting features!

Sharing also means contributing to the same pool of knowledge you once drew from, completing a beautiful learning cycle, building, and giving back. Whether it's a simple script or a complex AI system, every project adds value, inspiring and facilitating learning for others. This cycle of sharing and collaboration is what accelerates innovation in the AI field, pushing us all forward into new territories of possibility and discovery. So, dive into these projects with a novice's curiosity and a pioneer's fervor. Who knows—the project you share might be the spark that ignites someone else's passion for AI. That's how I ended up writing this book. Someone showed me a snippet of things to do when you have 8 hours in the Canary Islands.

Standing in the digital aisles of the vast AI marketplace can feel like choosing the right ice cream flavor at a new ice cream shop—overwhelming, exciting, and a bit of a gamble. You want to pick a tool that tastes great and doesn't melt into a puddle before you even get home. In AI terms, this means finding tools that are easy to use, scale with your needs, come with solid support, and align with your ethical values. Let's whip out our metaphorical taste-test spoons and examine how to evaluate AI products and tools.

Think about ease of use. This is like checking if you can actually pry open the ice cream tub without needing a chainsaw. This means intuitive interfaces, clear documentation, and a gentle learning curve for AI tools. It's vital because, let's be Smart, no one loves spending hours on setup or navigating through a labyrinthine interface to perform a simple task. Tools that prioritize ***user experience*** and have active user forums or clear guides score high on the usability scale.

Scalability is your next checkpoint. Just like you'd want a freezer big enough if you plan to stock up on that ice cream for the summer, you need AI tools that can grow with your needs. Whether it's processing larger datasets as you expand your projects or handling more complex algorithms, the tool should be able to scale up without major hiccups. Check for tools that offer different versions or upgrades, and look at reviews or case studies to see how they've handled growth for other users.

Support resources are crucial. Good AI tools come with solid support through detailed documentation, responsive customer service, or active community forums where you can get help from other users. This is especially important when starting, as even small roadblocks can seem impossible.

Community activity around the tool can also give you insights into its reliability and the richness of its ecosystem. A vibrant community means better support and more shared resources and indicates the tool's credibility and longevity in the market. It's like choosing a famous ice cream brand over a no-name one—you'll likely find more flavors (or plugins and add-ons), and it's probably popular for a reason.

Ethical Considerations in AI Tools

Now, let's talk about the ethical flavor of your AI tool—because no one wants their tech to leave a bad taste. You want strong security measures to protect your data from getting leaked or misused. When evaluating AI tools, look for those that adhere to robust security protocols and have transparent privacy policies. It's also wise to check for past security breaches and see how the company handled them.

Ethical implications are equally important. AI can be a double-edged sword, and it's important to consider how the tool handles data, especially if you're dealing with sensitive information. Look for tools designed with fairness in mind, ensuring that the AI doesn't perpetuate biases or cause harm. This includes checking the diversity of the data sets used for training the AI—more diverse data helps reduce bias.

Performing a Comparative Analysis

Choosing between AI tools can be daunting, but a comparative analysis can simplify this decision. Start by listing down your top choices based on the criteria we discussed. Create a comparison chart that includes ease of use, scalability, support, community activity, security, and ethical considerations. Rate each tool against these criteria based on your research—user reviews, product demos, and forum discussions can all be helpful sources of information.

For each tool, also consider how well it aligns with your specific needs and goals. If you're working on large data sets, scalability might weigh more heavily in your decision. If you're new to AI, then ease of use and strong support might be your top priorities. This tailored approach ensures that your chosen tool fits your personal or project requirements like a glove.

Staying Updated on AI Tools

AI technology evolves at breakneck speed, and staying updated can be a challenge—it's not impossible. Follow AI blogs and newsletters from reputable sources to keep a finger on the pulse of new developments. Joining specialized online communities can also provide insights into emerging tools and techniques. Keeping your knowledge fresh ensures you remain at the cutting edge of AI technology, ready to leverage the latest tools and techniques in your projects.

Embracing AI: Next Steps to Becoming an AI-Savvy Individual

Bringing AI into your daily life can start with something as simple as using smart home devices. These devices not only respond to your commands (like turning the lights off with a simple voice command), but they can also learn your preferences over time, adjusting the lighting or heating how you like it without ever having to lift a finger. But it's not just about comfort; it's about efficiency, too. AI-enhanced apps can help you manage your schedule, track your fitness regime, and even help you stick to your budget. In the workplace, AI-driven tools can automate repetitive tasks like data entry, schedule management, or customer inquiries, freeing you up to focus on your job's creative and strategic aspects.

As you rely more on AI, remember it's constantly evolving. This is where the importance of continual learning comes into play. Just as software needs updating to stay relevant, your knowledge and skills need regular refreshing if you want to stay ahead in the AI game. This doesn't mean burying yourself in books every weekend; instead, it's about staying curious and open to learning. Subscribe to AI newsletters, watch webinars, or take an online course now and then. Platforms like Coursera and edX regularly update their courses to reflect new developments in the field, allowing you to stay on the cutting edge without overwhelming you.

Don't keep all this knowledge to yourself. AI literacy is an invaluable asset, not just for you but for your community. Share what you've learned with friends, colleagues, or even through a blog. Organize a workshop or start a discussion group. Helping others understand AI demystifies the technology and fosters an informed and conscious community about how AI shapes our world. By advocating for AI literacy, you contribute to a society that approaches AI with wisdom and enthusiasm rather than fear and misunderstanding.

By integrating AI into your daily routines, continually educating yourself on new developments, being mindful of ethical considerations, and sharing your knowledge, you're not just keeping up with technology—you're shaping a future where AI enhances our lives with **integrity** and purpose. So, step forward with confidence and curiosity. After all, the future isn't just something that happens to us. We can shape it, one smart decision at a time.

When taking proactive steps toward becoming AI-savvy, remember that each small step is part of a more significant journey toward understanding AI and mastering how to coexist with these intelligent systems in ways that make our lives better. Looking forward, let's carry this blend of knowledge and ethical responsibility into exploring the broader impacts of AI in society, ensuring that as we advance technologically, we progress humanely and justly.

Chapter Nine

BONUS CONTENT

While researching this book, I discovered a device called Plaud, which someone used during a Zoom meeting with me. I had an "Aha" moment when I started my AI journey and was about to have another. I thought out loud, "...that's so cool. I wonder if it could help me." At that moment, I interrupted and asked a million questions like a four-year-old: What's that? What's it doing? How does it do that? No kidding!

I receive no compensation for any suggestion I have made. I should only be so fortunate.

This item captures calls, Zoom meetings, voice memos, and possibly more. As a publisher and an A-type personality, it's an absolute game-changer for me. I no longer have to take notes in meetings or transcribe my flowing streams of consciousness. After capturing a recording, a transcript, summary, and mind map are created. It takes a moment. Then, you have an electronic document you can edit, email, and add action items to; I never have to take another note, mostly.

Like ChatGPT, I balked at the price and had to do my research. It is a relatively new item. The tech community, which most are more tech-savvy than I am, is hashing it a bit, given they already know workarounds to produce the same result. I do not know those things they know, and out of the box, I am more effective. It frees up time, allowing for more wandering mind creativity. That's what I call day-dreaming with an intention.

Right out of the box, I downloaded an app and used it on a Zoom call I attended to check out the product. I missed the end of the presentation, so a short time later, I stopped the recording. The app informed me when the transcript was ready, and just like that, the entire meeting, including the parts I missed, was transcribed into a document I could manipulate, copy, and paste anywhere or save as a whole. I'll repeat it, what a game-changer for me.

Chapter Ten

Keeping the Journey Alive

Thank You!

    I want to take a moment to thank you for reading *AI for Beginners: Skeptics Guide to Automate Tasks, Streamline Your Life and Expand Your Earnings with Fun, Easy Exercises Anyone Can Do—NO TECH SKILLS Needed!*

Your journey into AI is just beginning, and I hope this book has given you the confidence to take the next step. Whether you're automating tasks, saving time, or looking to boost your earnings, I truly appreciate you allowing me to be a part of your learning adventure.

If you enjoyed the book or found it helpful, I'd be incredibly grateful if you could take a few minutes to leave a review on Amazon. Your feedback not only helps me as an author but also supports others who are looking for simple ways to get started with AI.

How to Leave a Review:
Click the QR code -

Or click/follow this link - https://a.co/d/6VJ6jW5

Every review makes a difference, and your support means the world to me!

Thank you again for reading, and I wish you continued success on your AI journey.

Warmly,

Tony Williams

Chapter Eleven

References

DataCamp. (n.d.). What is AI? A quick-start guide for beginners. https://www.datacamp.com/blog/what-is-ai-quick-start-guide-for-beginners

TechTarget. (n.d.). The history of artificial intelligence: Complete AI timeline. https://www.techtarget.com/searchenterpriseai/tip/The-history-of-artificial-intelligence-Complete-AI-timeline

NVIDIA. (n.d.). The difference between AI, machine learning, and deep learning. https://blogs.nvidia.com/blog/whats-difference-artificial-intelligence-machine-learning-deep-learning-ai/

upGrad. (n.d.). Neural networks: Applications in the real world. https://www.upgrad.com/blog/neural-networks-applications-in-the-real-world/

Marr, B. (2019, December 16). The 10 best examples of how AI is already used in our everyday life. Forbes. https://www.forbes.com/sites/bernardmarr/2019/12/16/the-10-best-examples-of-how-ai-is-already-used-in-our-everyday-life/

Office of the Victorian Information Commissioner. (n.d.). Artificial intelligence and privacy – Issues and chal-

lenges. https://ovic.vic.gov.au/privacy/resources-for organisations/artif
icial-intelligence-and-privacy-issues-and-challenges/

Investopedia. (n.d.). What is a virtual assistant, and what does one do?
https://www.investopedia.com/terms/v/virtual-assistant.asp#:~:text=
A%20virtual%20assistant%20helps%20with,their%20co%2Dworkers%
20or%20employers

Vector Security. (n.d.). Exploring the future impact of AI in home
security. https://www.vectorsecurity.com/exploring the future-impact
of ai in-home-security

The Tesseract Academy. (n.d.). Artificial intelligence in the creative
industries. https://tesseract.academy/artificial-intelligence-in-the-creat
ive-industries/

Henkin, D. (2023, December 5). Orchestrating the future—AI in the
music industry. Forbes. https://www.forbes.com/sites/davidhenkin/2
023/12/05/orchestrating-the-future-ai-in-the-music-industry/

Bootcamp. (n.d.). Application of artificial intelligence in art and design. https://bootcamp.uxdesign.cc/application-of-artificial-intelligen
ce-in-art-and-design-24ac861b7a4d

Marr, B. (2024, April 18). The role of generative AI in video game
development. Forbes. https://www.forbes.com/sites/bernardmarr/20
24/04/18/the-role-of-generative-ai-in-video-game-development/

Harvard Gazette. (2020, October). Ethical concerns mount as AI takes bigger decision-making
role. https://news.harvard.edu/gazette/story/2020/10/ethical-concern
s-mount-as-ai-takes-bigger-decision-making-role/

Transcend. (n.d.). Examining privacy risks in AI systems. https://tra
nscend.io/blog/ai-and-privacy

Berkeley Haas. (n.d.). Mitigating bias in artificial intelligence. https: //haas.berkeley.edu/equity/resources/playbooks/mitigating-bias-in-ai/

Nature. (n.d.). The impact of artificial intelligence on employment. https://www.nature.com/articles/s41599-024-02647-9#:~:text=AI%20 and%20machines%20increase%20labour,will%20emerge%20(Polak%20 2021)

Writesonic. (n.d.). Top 9 no-code AI chatbot builders: Know the ultimate. https://writesonic.com/blog/no-code-ai-chatbot-builder

Popular Photography. (n.d.). How to use AI to tag and organize your photo library. https://www.popphoto.com/how-to/tag-and-organize -photos-with-ai/

ZDNet. (n.d.). The best home automation systems of 2024. https://www.zdnet.com/home-and-office/smart-home/best-ho me-automation-system/

FitSW. (n.d.). Artificial intelligence in the fitness industry. https://w ww.fitsw.com/blog/artificial-intelligence-in-the-fitness-industry/

Resumely.ai. (n.d.). The role of artificial intelligence (AI) in career development. https://www.resumely.ai/blog/single/unlocking-su ccess-the-role-of-artificial-intelligence-ai-in-career-development

Liguori, M. (n.d.). Essential AI skills for non-technical professionals. LinkedIn. https://www.linkedin.com/pulse/essential-ai-skills-non -technical-professionals-new-economy-liguori--syecf

Raconteur. (n.d.). How four small businesses are making use of AI on a budget. https://www.raconteur.net/technology/four-ai-case-studies

National Center for Biotechnology Information. (n.d.). Ethical issues of artificial intelligence in medicine and healthcare. https://www.ncbi. nlm.nih.gov/pmc/articles/PMC8826344/

Reichental, J. (2023, November 20). Quantum artificial intelligence is closer than you think. Forbes. https://www.forbes.com/sites/jonathanreichental/2023/11/2 0/quantum-artificial-intelligence-is-closer-than-you-think/

LatentView. (n.d.). The intersection of AI and IoT: Use cases across industries. https://www.latentview.com/blog/the-intersection-of-ai-a nd-iot-use-cases-across-industries/

United Nations Environment Programme (n.d.). How artificial intelligence is helping tackle environmental challenges. https://www.unep.org/news-and-stories/story/how-artificial-i ntelligence-helping-tackle-environmental-challenges

IQVIA. (2024, February). The future of AI in healthcare. https://w ww.iqvia.com/blogs/2024/02/the-future-of-ai-in-healthcare

ProjectPro. (n.d.). 20 artificial intelligence project ideas for beginners [2024]. https://www.projectpro.io/article/artificial-intelligence-projec t-ideas/461

Medium. (n.d.). How to stay motivated when learning data science. https://medium.com/swlh/how-to-stay-motivated-when-learni ng-data-science-ccab719ae7c1

Unite.AI. (2024, July). 10 best AI tools for education (July 2024). https://www.unite.ai/10-best-ai-tools-for-education/

Harvard Gazette. (2020, October). Ethical concerns mount as AI takes bigger decision-making role. https://news.harvard.edu/gazette/story/2020/10/ethical-concerns-mo unt-as-ai-takes-bigger-decision-making-role/#:~:text=AI%20presents% 20three%20major%20areas,political%20implications%20of%20new%2 0technologies.

Business Wire. (2024, May 30) Paige delivers the power of foundation model technology to revolutionize pharmaceutical life science AI development. Business Wire. https://www.businesswire.com/news/home/20240530176318/en/Pai ge-Delivers-the-Power-of-Foundation-Model-Technology-to-Revolutio nize-Pharmaceutical-Life-Science-AI-Development

OpenAI. (2024). ChatGPT (4.0) [Large language model]. https://c hatgpt.com/c/bb8509b8-3a4d-49ee-b69b-1e8df446f591

OpenAI. (2024). ChatGPT (4.0) [Large language model]. https://c hatgpt.com/c/f090a69e-a362-4c88-8fe8-bb5083296220

Harvard Gazette. (2020, October 8). Ethical concerns mount as AI takes bigger decision-making role. Harvard Gazette. https://news.harvard.edu/gazette/story/2020/10/ethical-con cerns-mount-as-ai-takes-bigger-decision-making-role/

Category: Artificial Intelligence Artificial Intelligence – Impaxsys. h ttps://impaxsys.com/category/ai/

Businesswire   2024 https://www.businesswire.com/news/home/20240530176318/en/Pai ge-Delivers-the-Power-of-Foundation-Model-Technology-to-Revolutio nize-Pharmaceutical-Life-Science-AI-Development

OpenAI. (2024). *ChatGPT* (4o) [Large language model]. https://c hatgpt.com/c/bb8509b8-3a4d-49ee-b69b-1e8df446f591

OpenAI. (2024). *ChatGPT* (4o) [Large language model]. https://ch atgpt.com/c/f090a69e-a362-4c88-8fe8-bb5083296220

(2020). Artificial Intelligence and its Application in Various Fields. https://doi.org/10.35940/ijeat.D9144.069520

Made in United States
Orlando, FL
02 January 2025

56839377R00080